FIX IT
STAGE IT
SELL IT
QUICK!

FIX IT
STAGE IT
SELL IT
QUICK!

A DO-IT-YOURSELFER'S GUIDE
FOR **RAPID TURNOVER** OF ANY
HOME IN ANY **MARKET**

Robert Irwin

PUBLISHING

New York

Vice President and Publisher: Maureen McMahon
Editorial Director: Jennifer Farthing
Acquisitions Editor: Michael Sprague
Development Editor: Joshua Martino
Production Editor: Julio Espin
Production Designer: Todd Bowman
Cover Designer: Rod Hernandez

Published by Kaplan Publishing, a division of Kaplan, Inc.
1 Liberty Plaza, 24th Floor
New York, NY 10006

Printed in the United States of America
September 2007

07 08 09 10 9 8 7 6 5 4 3 2 1

ISBN 13: 978-1-4277-5474-5

Contents

Introduction

Sell It Fast!

Once you decide to sell your home, you probably want to move fast. After that decision to sell is made, most of us want to get it sold right now, today, quick!

After all, there's seldom any advantage in taking a long time to sell. Homes on the market more than a month or so tend to be considered "stale," and agents often overlook them when selecting properties to show. Buyers think there's something wrong with these stale properties because they haven't sold quicker, which encourages them to make lower offers. And as the homes stay on the market even longer, investors see them as low-balling opportunities—a chance to "steal" a home.

On the other hand, you, as a seller, have to keep maintaining the property at peak appearance, make the monthly payments, and delay moving to that next home you want.

Of course, you don't want any of this. You want your home sold quickly, don't you?

But, you don't want to give it away. Any agent will tell you that you can get a quick sale simply by lowering your price far enough. Get it sufficiently low and even the agent will buy the place! All the world loves a bargain.

Yes, you want a quick sale, but you also want a good price, hopefully the top price your home can bring. Hence, selling your home quickly is not your only goal. Your other goal is getting top dollar for that home.

The real question is how do you get *both*—a quick sale *and* top dollar? There are the five elements to every quick sale for top dollar:

1. Fix up the property.
2. Stage the property.
3. Develop a marketing plan.
4. Hire the optimum agent (selling "by owner" is discussed in Chapter 13).
5. Price it right.

We'll consider all five in detail as you go through this book. But, let's briefly look at them, here:

Fix Up and Stage the Property

Everyone knows, or ought to know, the most important factor in determining price for a home is location. (Remember the 3Ls in real estate? "Location, Location, Location!")

As a seller there's not much you can do about your home's location. After all, you can't very well move it to a better neighborhood.

But, you can do something about your home's condiction. That's the second most important factor in determining price. It's also an important factor in determining how quickly you get the place sold.

The condition of your home is what buyers see when they tour it. By the time they come by, presumably they already know the location and have decided that it's acceptable. If you're within the buyer's price range and desired location, then it's up to your house to sell itself. If the house shows well, you should get an offer. If it shows badly, the buyers will likely move on.

Thus, as a seller, getting your price and a quick sale mainly comes down to how well your home "shows."

The Elements of Showing

There are just two things you can do to improve the way your home shows: fix it up . . . and stage it.

Fixing up your home means what it says: fixing anything and everything that's broken. It means bringing your home back up to the condition it was in when it was brand new.

Staging means something different. Staging means dressing up your home. Think of it in terms of people. When a couple goes to a ball, in order to shine, the woman wears a lovely dress and accessories, has her hair done, uses makeup, applies perfume, and so on. A man wears a fine suit, perhaps a tux, shines his shoes, makes sure his hair is neat and trimmed, and so on. If done right, the couple will get gasps of appreciation from others there. They'll get noticed. Their appearance will, in effect, sell them to the crowd.

With a home, it's something similar. You stage the home by simple things such as adding flowers and plants and by removing clutter. You can also do more sophisticated things such as installing better lighting and even renting more appropriate furnishings. (We'll have far more to say about staging in the second section of this book.)

When you've gotten your home all fixed up and properly staged, it's ready to be seen by buyers. If done right, they will appreciate its appearance, some even going to the extent of falling in love with it. And that will result in high offers, quick!

Selling It

Of course, you also need to promote your home effectively by hiring a good agent (or learning to do the work yourself ala FSBO [for sale by owner]), getting a marketing plan, and going through all the steps involved in selling any real estate.

We'll cover what you need to know to promote your home in the last section of this book.

Get It Sold—Quick!

But what's a "quick" sale?

In a normal market where homes take anywhere from three to four months to sell, a quick sale would be getting a buyer to make an offer you can accept within the first 30 days, preferably within the first week. Of course, if the market is slow, it's going to take a little longer. On the other hand, in a super-hot market, as was the case a few years ago, it could be only a few days or hours to a quick sale.

Want a quick sale (for top dollar)?

Then follow the five elements noted earlier. Don't be a seller who simply does nothing and waits around for that perfect buyer to come and offer a high price. Chances are you'll be waiting a very long time.

Instead, get off your duff and shine up your home. Oh, and a word about cost. Yes, it will cost you something to adequately prepare your home for sale. Usually the cost is small, a few thousand dollars. Sometimes, however, if the home has severe problems, it could cost more.

Whatever the cost, though, fixing up and staging are a necessary part of the sales process. If you want to get the highest price and the quickest sale, you have to do the work. (If you don't have the money, short-term financing to assist in preparing your home is readily available — see Chapter 5.) And remember, the money you spend on getting your home ready isn't thrown away. You should earn back that money (and more!) when you sell.

Want a quick sale for the highest price your home can bring? Turn the page and get started!

Fix It!

1 Curb Appeal—First Impressions Are Everything . . . Almost!

WE'VE ALL HEARD the expression that you never get a second chance to make a good first impression. It's true: first impressions are critical—and not only when meeting people but also when meeting houses. Buyers form a first impression of a home as soon as they drive up (or are driven up by an agent). If that first impression is good, the house is half sold. If it's bad, then you and/or your agent will spend the next half hour trying to reverse that bad impression, just to get back to the buyer's neutral position.

How the buyer first sees your house is called *curb appeal,* or in the case of a house that looks bad, *lack of curb appeal.*

KEY CONCEPT *Curb appeal applies not only to the outside of your home but to the buyer's first impression of the interior—when he or she first opens the door and walks in; when the buyer first sees your living room, kitchen, master bedroom and bath, and all the other rooms of your house. That first impression, whether good or bad, is remembered and is crucial when getting a sale and a better price.*

Curb appeal is such a well-known concept in real estate that on the surface, almost no one argues with it. Most sellers simply say, "Of course, it's obvious," *and then go on to ignore it.*

I've repeatedly seen sellers refuse to do elementary things to fix up and stage their property—things that any real estate agent would tell them are important. Things as simple as keeping the front lawn mowed and the hedges trimmed, as straightforward as cleaning the toilets and keeping dirty pots and pans out of the sink and off the counter, as undemanding as removing clutter, and on and on.

In a fast-paced market, such as we've seen in most areas over the past few years, sellers could sometimes get away with this. When buyers were lined up to make offers on any home that was for sale, first impressions could sometimes be overlooked. I witnessed buyers who made offers *sight-unseen* on homes, sometimes offering more than the asking price! (On the other hand, fixing and staging homes became more prevalent during that same hot market when savvy sellers realized that doing just the right amount of work could get a significantly higher price.)

Of course, times change. Today, with a more normal, or even a slow market in many areas plus finicky buyers, curb appeal has never been more important. Today, the appearance of the home can make all the difference between getting a good price and a quick sale or having the home languish on the market, only receiving low-ball offers.

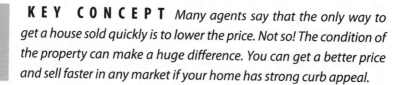

KEY CONCEPT *Many agents say that the only way to get a house sold quickly is to lower the price. Not so! The condition of the property can make a huge difference. You can get a better price and sell faster in any market if your home has strong curb appeal.*

If curb appeal is so important, why would any seller ignore it? The reason is that often it's inconvenient for sellers to deal with curb appeal. To improve the curb appeal of your home you might have to do many things, including:

- Paint your home inside and out.
- Put in a new lawn and driveway.
- Install a new front door, or at least paint the old one.
- Plant new shrubs and flowers.
- Clean old carpeting or install new carpeting.
- Repair and improve kitchen and baths (beyond simply cleaning).
- Fix all broken items.

We'll delve into all the things that you need to fix and stage to make a better first impression throughout this book.

To improve the curb appeal of your home, you may have to spend time and *money*. And the last thing that sellers want to do is to spend money on a home they are planning to move out of. They frequently reason that money spent on improving a home before a sale only benefits the buyer. After all, it's the buyer who moves in and enjoys the improvements!

That's faulty reasoning. Improving the curb appeal of your home benefits you, the seller, in two important ways:

1. It will result in your getting a higher price for the property.
2. It can get you a quicker sale.

Further, as we'll see in the first two parts of this book, you probably won't need to spend a great deal of money. Those fixes and stagings that most improve curb appeal are almost always the least expensive. Often, improving the curb appeal of your home can be done for as little as a thousand dollars, sometimes less! (Of course, it could take more, if the condition of your property is seriously bad and if there's lots of deferred maintenance.)

Which brings us to another very important concept when selling your home:

K E Y   C O N C E P T *Cost does not equate with value.*

I believe this is a concept that we all intuitively understand. But, many of us simply refuse to accept its consequences.

I know a seller, Rachel, whose furnace went out in the middle of last winter. Rachel was planning to sell in the spring in the $300,000 range and knew she could never sell with a broken furnace. Further, she had no intention of being cold over the winter.

So, Rachel called in a heating/air conditioning specialist who told her that it would cost around a $1,000 to fix the old unit. But more important, the old system was 20 years old and very inefficient. He said that new furnaces/air conditioners were nearly one-third more efficient, thus saving her 33 percent or more in fuel and electricity costs. The new system would pay for itself in less than a decade. And during that time, she would enjoy a warmer house in winter and a cooler one in summer.

But, she complained, she was planning to sell in a few months.

Even better, the salesman said. Think of how impressed buyers would be when told that the home had a brand-new, more efficient furnace and air conditioner. People today are very sensitive to the high costs of heating and cooling, he said. Many are concerned about wasting energy. They'll jump at the chance to buy and pay far more than the cost of the new system! (Wrong!)

So, Rachel decided to bite the bullet and put in a complete new system, including furnace, air conditioner, and ductwork—at a cost of about $8,500.

The salesperson was right about two things: her home was definitely warmer in winter (and probably would be cooler when summer came). And her heating bills did drop, though not quite by a third.

Where he was wrong was when it came to how much more *value* the new system added to the house. Although she and her agent touted the new furnace/air conditioner to every buyer who came by, the fact was that she was in competition with every other home in her neighborhood. Two of those for sale didn't have new furnaces/air conditioners and both of which, as a result, were selling for thousands of dollars less. Because Rachel raised her price by the

$8,500 she spent to get back her cost of putting in the new system, she was now significantly higher in price than the other properties.

What she discovered was that, yes, buyers did like the new furnace/cooling system. But, they figured every house came with such a system, so why should they pay more for it? They figured that maybe a more efficient system was worth a few more dollars on the price, but no buyer was willing to pay $8,500 more. Eventually, she sold for a competitive price—and figured that she had eaten at least $5,000 to $6,000 of the cost of the new heater/air conditioner. If she had simply spent $1,000 to repair the old system, she wouldn't have lost the money out of her pocket.

The important lesson she learned was that the cost of fixing up the property, in this case, did not equate with value. Your fixing-up cost does not automatically add equity to your home.

Unfortunately, Rachel is not alone. Well more than half of sellers I've known fall into this trap. They feel that if they spend the money on fixing up their home, they'll automatically get it back out when they sell. Statistics indicate quite the opposite. With the exception of some makeovers of kitchens and baths (which we'll discuss in later chapters), you *almost never* get your money out when you fix up a home. Indeed, most fixes yield *less than half* of what they cost.

Why?

For the answer we have to go back to curb appeal. Rachel, the seller in our example, fixed a part of her home that in no way contributed to the first impression made on a buyer. Buyers rarely spend any time at all looking at the furnace or air conditioner, other than to make sure that the home has one and that it works.

Thus, our seller's mistake was in assuming that buyers would pay for something they couldn't see. Buyers simply *did not equate value with the cost* the seller paid for something unseen. I call it a lack of "visual value."

This applies across the board to items that are not visible. The kinds of things that you can waste money on when fixing your home up for sale because their cost does not equate with value is legendary, and we'll go into them in detail in the next chapter. But first, let's look at another important concept about the curb appeal of your home. Again, it's simple-minded, but so often overlooked that it needs emphasis.

Fix Everything That's Broken

I once was buying a home for investment. (You'll sometimes get buyers who want to purchase your property not to live in themselves, but to rent out. While they seldom pay top price, they often will offer a very quick sale.) As I toured the home I tried the light switch in one of the bedrooms. It sparked, then connected, and then the light went on. A moment later, it sparked and the light went out.

"Bad switch," I said.

The owner appeared a little embarrassed but said nothing.

Because of the incident, I tried all the switches in all the rooms and found one in the dining room that seemed to work nothing. It was a dead switch. "Bad electrical system," I said. Again the owner seemed a bit embarrassed but said nothing.

When I made my offer, I cut my price $11,000 below what I would otherwise have offered and told the seller it was because I might need to rewire the entire home.

The seller was appalled. "There's nothing wrong with the electrical system," he pleaded. "The house is only 25 years old."

"Maybe, maybe not." I replied, and then reminded him of the bad switches. I also insisted on a thorough inspection of the property. The final sales price dropped by $5,000 because of my concerns, even though an inspector eventually found that the only thing wrong was a few bum switches.

Don't let a buyer do to you what I did to that seller simply because you didn't fix something that was broken. If the seller had simply fixed two switches, he would have saved $5,000 in lost equity. The switches together probably cost less than $3.

Just as cost does not equate with value when you have something fixed, neither does it equate with value when you don't fix something that's evidently and conspicuously broken.

Remember that just because you're willing to live with something broken, don't assume any buyers will feel the same way. Even if the buyers never use it, they will want it in working condition when they take over the property.

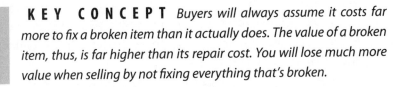

KEY CONCEPT *Buyers will always assume it costs far more to fix a broken item than it actually does. The value of a broken item, thus, is far higher than its repair cost. You will lose much more value when selling by not fixing everything that's broken.*

While you might get away with something that's broken and isn't seen (such as a bad attic fan) by promising to fix it before the deal closes, that won't work with anything that a buyer can see (or switch or turn on). When a buyer sees something that doesn't work, he or she automatically makes a reduction in the offering price. And that reduction, as noted, is almost always far in excess of the actual cost of fixing the problem.

Do Cosmetic Fixes First

All of which leads us back to visual value: fix that which can be seen first (and perhaps only). Fix everything that a buyer can see. Don't spend a lot of time worrying about what buyers can't see. Let's take another example to be sure the point is made.

A friend recently sold a home in California that had a cracked slab and a pool with cracked cement around it. For those unfamiliar with construction, it's quite common to have slabs of cement in the Southwest. And almost any cement will crack, at least in small hairline cracks, over time.

In many Southwest houses, a peripheral foundation is placed in the ground and then a slab of concrete 4 to 6 inches thick is placed inside it. The walls and ceiling are supported by the peripheral foundation, while the slab serves as the actual floor. (Needless to say, there are very few basements in the Southwest!)

For a pool, a slab of concrete is typically placed all round it. This helps keep water away from the dirt at the side of the pool. (Standing water on the outside of the pool can have bad effects over time.)

As noted, however, cement has a habit of cracking, even under the best of circumstances. Hairline cracks are quite common. Larger cracks that go all the way through a slab are not uncommon, especially in areas with expansive (clay) soil. That's why reinforcing bars (rebars) of steel are put into slabs, to keep them from shifting if (mostly "when") they crack.

Nevertheless, a cracked slab is a cracked floor and, in this case, a cracked pool walk-around. In the home, it potentially could mean lots of serious problems, including cracked walls and ceilings and, in the worst scenario, a house that's ready to fall down. With the pool walk-around, it's less problematic, especially when the pool itself does not have a crack in it.

So, my friend had a house to sell with two cracked slabs—one in the house and the other around the pool.

However, the house had wall-to-wall carpeting, which completely covered over the inside cracks. Thus, the eventual buyer *could not easily see them*. Of course, the cracks by the pool were perfectly evident.

That does not mean any cracks were kept a secret. When a sale was made, my friend, the seller, disclosed the internal slab cracks in writing. The buyers asked their home inspector about it. The home inspector said she couldn't report on anything that was not visible, including problems in walls and under wall-to-wall carpet that was tacked down. But, she said that such cracks were common and usually not a serious problem.

The buyers accepted this. However, it was a different story when it came to the cracks around the pool. Although they were tiny and probably of far less consequence, they were *visible*. The buyers could see them and, as a result, insisted on a price reduction because of the loss of value they felt the cracks caused.

Be sure you understand the story correctly. The buyers did not object to potentially more serious cracks in the slab under the house and did not insist on a price reduction for them, because they *could not see* them. The buyers, however, did object to the probably insignificant cracks in the cement around the pool and did insist on a price reduction because they *could see* them. To make the sale, my friend had to reduce the price because of the pool slab, but not because of the cracked slab in the house.

The moral of the story is that what the buyers did *not* see did not reduce the value of the property. What they *could* see did adversely affect price.

This is not to say that the buyers bought a bad house or that the seller sold something in an underhanded way. Everything was disclosed, and chances are the cracks in both the interior and pool slabs were indeed minor and never will bother the buyer. However, perception is key to value. Thus, the rule is that when fixing up property, you should do whatever is necessary to fix anything that's visible. In other words, do all cosmetic fixes. Remember, it's a matter of *visual value*.

Avoid "As Is" Sales

One last point regarding curb appeal needs to be mentioned and that has to do with "as is" sales. Some sellers feel they can avoid fixing things that detract from the curb appeal of their property by offering to sell it "as is." This means that the buyers agree to take the property in whatever condition it's in, without making any demands on the seller to fix it up. Of course, the seller is normally still required to reveal any defects in the property just as if it were sold without being "as is."

 K E Y   C O N C E P T *Always try to avoid "as is" sales because they will yield you a much lower price. "As is," in buyers' minds, equates with a loss of value, and their offering price will reflect that.*

The problem is that as soon as buyers hear those two words, *as is*, they assume something is drastically wrong with the property.

They assume the worst. They assume that there's something wrong that the seller hasn't disclosed (and even that a home inspection may not reveal). And then they offer accordingly in price.

Harvey, one seller I knew, simply didn't want to spend the time or money in painting his home, even though it had been a decade or longer since the home had been painted. It looked shabby and run-down. Similarly, Harvey didn't want to put in new carpeting to replace or even clean the worn and stained old carpeting inside. Those two items would have cost him several thousands of dollars, and he just didn't want to spend the money (even though an agent told Harvey he could get a short-term home equity loan to cover the costs; we'll discuss this in Chapter 5).

Thus, even though there was nothing major wrong with his home, he sold it "as is." Harvey said, "I want the buyers to know that I'm not doing anything to fix up this house. They want it; then what they see is what they get. I won't even accept any offers contingent upon repairs."

Indeed. What they saw was bad paint and bad carpeting. What they didn't see, however, worried them even more. As noted, in an "as is" sale, the seller is supposed to disclose everything that's wrong with the property (in those states where disclosures are statutory and elsewhere when buyers demand them as a contingency of the sale). Selling "as is" doesn't remove the seller from his or her disclosure responsibilities. But, buyers always assume that because the seller has chosen to sell "as is," there must be some hidden problems that aren't being disclosed. And, in order not to get caught paying too much for a home with a hidden (undisclosed) defect, buyers virtually always offer far lower.

In Harvey's case, there were two buyers who made offers, and in both cases they deducted not only the cost of replacing the carpeting and repainting the house, but they also deducted another 12 percent in one case and 10 percent in another off the fair market value of the home. (Fair market value [FMV] is determined by a comparative market analysis and is explained in Chapter 11.) These added deductions were precautions that the buyers felt they had to take simply because the house was being offered "as is." In other words, unless they could get a bargain on the property, the buyers weren't willing to take a chance on buying a "pig in a poke." They simply weren't willing to take the risk without being compensated with a lower price.

All of which is to say that stubbornly refusing to fix a problem in a home and instead attempting to get around it by selling "as is" is no real solution at all. It's sort of like jumping out of the frying pan and into the fire. In Harvey's case, he eventually took the home off the market for a few weeks, painted it, and put in inexpensive new carpeting. He also staged the property and then was able to quickly resell for the top of his price range without resorting to "as is." Like other sellers, he had to bite the bullet and do the necessary fix-up work to get a fair price.

Conclusion

Curb appeal and visual value as we've described here are important facts of life when selling real estate. It's not something you can choose to ignore. It happens no matter what you do. Buyers will make gut choices on the basis of what they first see and perceive. And in many cases, once your property has made an impression on that buyer, it's all but impossible to change it. (I've seen agents literally spend hours trying to show buyers how a property makes great financial and practical sense for them, all to no avail because their initial impression was so negative.)

You want to sell your home for a good price, and sell it quickly? Then pay attention to its curb appeal. Doll that property up to the point where a buyer falls in love with it, and your good sale will happen. (In books I've written aimed at buyers, I always tell them to *never fall in love* with a property—they should always have alternative homes to choose from. The reason is that buyers who fall in love with homes—just what you want—always pay too much. Think about it!)

Relative Importance of First Impressions
of Different Areas of a Home to Most Buyers

Rank	Area
1.	Curb appeal of front of home
2.	"Show" of interior of home
3.	Kitchen
4.	Master bathroom
5.	Living areas (living room, den, etc.)
6.	Master bedroom
7.	Other bathrooms
8.	Other bedrooms
9.	Backyard
10.	Garage
11.	Interior hallways

2 How Much Should You Do?

WHAT EVERY SELLER wants is to get back $2 for every $1 spent on fixing up his or her property. (Or maybe it's $10 back for every $1 spent!) Much of the time this isn't going to happen. But, one way to make it happen is to do the cosmetic work first. The best example of this is painting.

Buy a few gallons of paint and put them on both the exterior and interior of your house (assuming you don't do a sloppy job!) and you'll have added multiples of the paint's cost. Even if you hire a painter, chances are you'll get back much more than you spend here than anywhere else. Paint is the ultimate cosmetic fixer.

How Much Bang Will You Get Your for Your Bucks?

Going beyond paint, ideally you'll want to get at least as much back as you spend fixing up your property for sale. Whether that happens, of course, depends on the condition of your property, which fixes you choose to do, and how much money you spend on them.

For example I recently saw a home owner who was living in a 3-bedroom, 1-bath home. She recognized that having only one bathroom was holding her home back. So, at a cost of $30,000, she converted an unused closet into another bathroom. This so improved the appeal of her house that she was able to ask and get $43,000 more on a quick sale. With one bath, few buyers were interested. With two baths, there was a world of buyers who wanted the home. The fix added more value than the cost.

Unfortunately, that tends to be the exception and not the rule. In too many cases, it simply costs so much to do fix-up work that you can't recoup the cost in added value. (If, however, it speeds up the sale, you may still find it worthwhile.)

Let's look at some rules to follow to get the most value for the money.

Money Saving Fix-Up Rules

1. If It Isn't Broken, Don't Fix It!

Fixing a house implies that it's *broken*. (You don't want to fix something that isn't broken!) Most homes that are more than a few years old (and occasionally even brand new homes) have some things that are broken. These should be fixed *before* putting your home up for sale.

KEY CONCEPT *Fixing means repairing something that's busted. Staging means preparing the home for sale so that it looks its best. The difference is between repairing a broken faucet or adding a colorful soap dish, between putting in a new sink and cleaning up all dishes in an existing sink. (Although fixing and staging do overlap in some areas, in general we'll cover fixes in this section and get into staging in the next.)*

As we saw in the last chapter, If there are items in your home that need repair, and you don't do the work, then your home will take longer to sell and very likely will command a lower price. Failing to fix something busted should not be an option.

Some homes have so many broken items that they may be classified as a "fixer upper" or a "handyman special." These are rundown properties that, when not fixed up, show very badly. As a result, buyers make low-ball offers for them, deducting from the price what they (buyers) estimate it will cost to make the repairs. (Remember, buyers always figure more than the real costs, allowing for error and sometimes for their own profit.)

For example, I have a standing disagreement with my wife over what constitutes a "fixer." We frequently are out there looking at homes. Whenever she sees a home where the paint isn't perfect, where there's a mark or two on the carpeting, where the kitchen has a cracked tile in the countertop or has a few scratches in the floor, she refers to it as a "fixer." Then I step in and say that in my opinion, it's not a fixer. The house just needs some cleaning, painting, and rejuvenating. In my opinion, a home that's a true fixer has a serious problem, such as a cracked foundation, leaking roof, structural damage, or something similar. (See my book, *Find It, Buy It, Fix It,* for more information on true fixers!)

Regardless which of us is right in this argument, the seller of the home *always loses.* While an investor, such as myself, is more likely to see the property from my perspective, most buyers have my wife's perspective. More people see homes as my wife does than as I do. If buyers see *anything at all* wrong, they think of the home as a fixer. And as a fixer, they'll feel it warrants a low-ball price.

That's not a position you want to put yourself into.

In short, if buyers see every little thing as cause for lowering the price, from the seller's (your) perspective it only makes sense to fix every little thing, no matter how small the defect.

KEY CONCEPT *If you want to get your best price and quickest sale, you have to make sure you don't give a buyer the slightest opportunity to run down your property. You have to fix everything that needs repair.*

2. Repair Only the Part That's Broken

How much repair should you do?

Sometimes it's hard to tell. On the one hand, if you've got a broken window, it needs to be fixed. That's it—that's the minimum. No buyer is going to overlook a broken window. On the other hand, what if your home has an "adequate" kitchen. But it's old and outdated—obsolete. It was put in perhaps 30 years ago. The tiles have an old-fashioned yellow color, but only a few are cracked. The avocado green appliances are definitely out of style, but they work. The white sink has some stains and chips in it, but it's fully functional.

Do you spend the bucks to modernize the entire kitchen? Or do you do a minimal job just touching up stains, cracks, and breaks here and there? My answer is to do the minimum to bring the home up to the current neighborhood "norm" (see below).

3. Repair Up to Neighborhood Norms

When fixing up isn't a clear issue, a good way to decide what and how much to do is to consider neighborhood norms. In most cases where obsolescence is the big issue (as it often is in kitchens and bathrooms), how much fixing up you can justify should be determined not by your budget (you can always finance short-term repairs paid for by the subsequent sale; see Chapter 5), not by your own preferences (remember, you're preparing this house for a buyer other than you), nor by modern styles (as flashed on TV and decorating magazines), but by what your neighbors have done to their homes.

Yes, this is a case where your neighbor knows best.

The reason for this seemingly strange comparison (your house compared with your neighbors) is because price is determined in real estate by comparisons. When a licensed appraiser, or an agent, or a buyer comes to see your home and asks him- or herself what it's really worth, the first thing he or she will do (or should do) is to take a look at the "comps." These are properties *comp*arable to yours that have recently sold.

The recent (going back six months to a year) comps can be very revealing. If a single comp (home similar to yours) sold for $300,000, then it stands to reason that your home should sell for around $300,000 too. (It's the same principle as ketchup in the grocery store: if one brand's bottle sells for $2, then a comparable bottle by a different brand should likewise sell for around $2.)

Of course, prices tend to fall into a range. Typically, there are a number of homes similar to yours that have sold within a price range. For example, while one home might have sold for $300,000, other comps might have sold for $250,000 to $350,000. (Sometimes the sales are clumped together narrowly—$290,000 to $310,000—indicating all the homes are very similar.)

Of course, you as a seller want to get the top of the price range, not the bottom. The difference in our extreme example between $250,000 and $350,000 is $100,000. That $100,000 worth of difference is a lot of money.

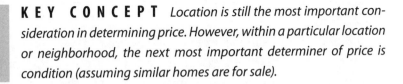

K E Y   C O N C E P T   *Location is still the most important consideration in determining price. However, within a particular location or neighborhood, the next most important determiner of price is condition (assuming similar homes are for sale).*

What separates the home that sold for the most from the home that sold from the least?

Assuming they're true comps (same number of bedrooms, bathrooms, comparable lot size and location, similar square footage, and so on), the difference usually comes down to *condition.*

The top house was in far better shape, and showed much better, than the bottom house. In other words, the top house was fixed up; the bottom house wasn't.

Thus, to get the top dollar in the price range for your location, you have to be sure that your home's condition is as good or better than any other comparable home for sale. Of course, you don't need to spend so much money and do so much work that your home *exceeds* the condition of its comps. But, you don't want to do so little that it shows *worse* than its comps.

4. Prepare for Savvy Buyers and Agents

Some sellers assume, or at least hope, that buyers won't really know about the competing homes for sale in the neighborhood (and elsewhere). That's a false hope. Today's buyers and agents are very savvy. A good agent will take a buyer to see all the comparable homes. Some agents will even take a buyer to an unfixed home just to demonstrate how much better a comp may look. (It's not entirely ethical, but it's done.) You don't want your home to be the one that's always shown to demonstrate to buyers what an unfixed house looks like!

Thus, you should expect buyers to fully know how your home compares with others for sale (and recently sold). If it shows well, it compares well. As a result, buyers will respond well to it. If it shows badly, it compares badly. Buyers will ignore it or make low-ball offers.

Let's take an example from a neighborhood near mine. The house next door to me was for sale. Looking at the comps, buyers quickly realized that all those homes that sold in the high part of the price range had a made-over kitchen. Those that sold lowest had nothing done to their old, existing kitchen. My neighbor had done nothing to his kitchen. Where in the price range do you think his house sold? (The bottom.) And how long do you think it took to sell? (Six and a half months, in a fairly strong market!)

5. Aim for the Top of Your Home's Price Range

You want a quick sale at a high price? Then let the comps and the neighborhood norms be your guide. If most of your neighbors have gone ahead and fixed up their kitchens and baths, to get the best price you'll have to do it too. In fact, if you don't do likewise, it will adversely affect the price you get for your property—you'll get toward the bottom of the range, or perhaps even set a new bottom. And your house will languish on the market.

Aim for the best price you can get, the top of the price range established by previous comps. Indeed, aim for setting a new top!

> **KEY CONCEPT** *Don't let buyers know more about your neighborhood than you do. Find out what the comps are for your home from an agent; then go visit the houses yourself. (Any agent will be happy to show you other properties to educate you to the market, all in the hope that you'll either list or buy from them.)*

6. Spend as Little as Possible

One last point on this topic: you don't need to spend as much as your neighbors did to bring your house up to the neighborhood norm. While your neighbors may have spent $50,000 on their kitchen makeovers, you may be able to cleverly get just as much punch for $15,000. We'll see how later.

You want to evaluate each fix-up project carefully to determine how much value you'll get for the cost. Sometimes you can do a minimal amount of work at a minimal cost and still get just as much "show."

7. Get a Professional Opinion

As noted, if it's a window that's broken, or there's a hole in the wall, or the paint is scratched and marred, fix it yourself or hire someone to do it. You shouldn't need someone to tell you what to do.

However, when it's more difficult to tell, and you're not sure about the neighborhood norms, then calling in a professional can help. Find an agent who "farms" your neighborhood and ask his or her opinion. (Most agents pick one or two neighborhoods and make it their business to know everything about them and to specialize in listing homes in them; in the trade it's called "farming.")

In addition, and especially if you have an older home, it should pay to get a good professional home inspection. You'll get some surprising information about what's broken and what's not. And, after you've fixed up the work, you can always show the report to buyers explaining that you've done all necessary fix-up work.

The best professional inspectors are often people who've previously worked in the building trades or worked for local governments as building inspectors. They also should belong to both national and state trade organizations. For more information you can check out:

- *www.nachi.org*
  National Association of Certified Home Inspectors
- *www.ashi.org*
  American Society of Home Inspectors
- *www.nahi.org*
  National Association of Home Inspectors

3 Projects That Build Equity and Buyer Enthusiasm

NOW, LET'S TAKE at look at your house and decide what to fix, how to fix it, and how much to spend. We'll start with the exterior front of the house, much as a buyer would, then move indoors.

Front Yard

Lawn—Cost: $100 if in OK shape; $1,500+ to sod

Your front yard should look sterling—a regular showcase of the property. After all, it's one of the first things that a buyer will see. That means that if you have a front lawn, it should be green with no brown or bare patches. If you have these, fix the lawn. Add extra water, fertilizer, and replant as needed for a few weeks before showing the property. And be sure that you keep it well mowed.

Hedges—Cost: $25 to trim

Hedges are a different matter. If you have extensive hedges that screen the house from the street, consider having them removed entirely. People like to see the property they are driving up to (curb appeal), and large hedges are sometimes distracting. While each case is different, I prefer to err on the side of making the house more visible. At the least, I suggest you trim the hedges way back, especially if they are towering and overgrown.

Trees—Cost: $250 to $1,200 each to remove

Trees that provide shade (beware of fruit trees that make a mess from dropped fruit) can be nice, but they must compliment the home. A palm tree or pine that looked cute when it was 3 feet tall will overshadow a home when it's 60 feet tall, especially if it's only a single-story property. Consider having too-tall trees removed. Yes, it's expensive, but removing them will often help the house look better in proportion to the lot.

Debris—Cost: $50 to $150 to have removed

Clean any debris away from the front. Don't stuff it on the side of the house; get rid of it at the dump. Debris makes the house look sloppy and cheap. Don't leave any of it behind!

Cement and Asphalt—Cost: $50 to $300 to repair; $3,500+ to replace

Clean your driveway and walkways. Remember, these are huge areas, and people look at them first. With asphalt, you often can inexpensively fill any cracks and put a new coating on it. This will improve the front's appearance enormously.

With cement, there are many different chemicals you can use to clean it, and most stains can be removed. Cracks, however, are a different matter. If the cracks are minor, my suggestion is to forget about them. Any attempts to fix them will only make them stand out.

If they are major, you can try several different solutions. If there are only a few long cracks, you can have a *cement cutting company* cut out straight strips where the cracks are (check the phone book or Internet; they'll come out to your house with a diamond-bladed cement saw and do the work in an hour or so for a few hundred dollars). You can then replace the strips with bricks. If done cleverly, a nice design can be created that looks perfectly natural. Otherwise, you're probably going to have to remove the old badly cracked cement and replace it. Because cement is so costly these days, you may want to consider replacing with asphalt. But, keep in mind the neighborhood norms. If every other house has a cement driveway, you'd better replace yours with cement as well, or you'll have your price dinged.

House Front

Paint—Cost: $200 do it yourself; $1,500 to hire out

If it's been a year since your home was last painted, repaint at least the front. You can do it yourself on a weekend with a few gallons of paint. It will make an enormous difference. And be sure to do the trim with a high-quality gloss paint so it stands out properly.

Flowers—Cost: $125+

This is one of the least expensive ways to create a colorful and beautiful house front. Buy "color pots" at nurseries and place them along the entrance to your home. Plant colorful flora in any bedding areas in front. Be sure to do this several weeks before showing your home, and water well. By the time you show, the front of your home can be a gorgeous garden of color.

In winter in parts of the country where the weather is inclement (snow, cold, and rain), of course, you'll have to avoid this touch. But be sure that you at least keep your driveway and entrance plowed, clear, and safe with anti-slip compounds.

Front Door—Cost: $150 to paint/stain; $1,500+ to replace

If it's a painted door, repaint it. Ideally, you'll put in one of those very beautiful stained wood doors with glass inserts. However, they are costly and could push your home above neighborhood norms. (If every one on the block has a beautiful stained wood door with glass, your home will be dinged by buyers if you don't have one too.) You can find a broad range of new doors at stores like Home Depot and Lowe's. Just be sure you have them professionally installed; you don't want a front door that doesn't fit right, creaks when it opens, or doesn't close properly.

If your home is more than a year old, put new hardware (handle, lock, eyehole, etc.) on the front door(s). The hardware that comes with the home is often inexpensive and fades or corrodes quickly. Even new inexpensive hardware will look terrific for at least six months. And it usually costs less than $50.

Clean Front Windows—Cost: $10 do it yourself; $150 hire out

Clean them, including the sills. If the screens are faded or torn, replace them.

Kitchen Makeover
Total Cost: $2,500 TO $50,000+

For most buyers, the kitchen is the most important room in the house. Many people buy homes based on how the kitchen looks. If your kitchen is the sort of place that a buyer falls in love with, you've probably got a quick, high-priced sale.

Yet, it's so hard to put a definitive price tag on a kitchen make-over because so much depends on what shape it currently is in, on how much work is done, and what quality materials are chosen. In some cases to justify the costs, you'll only want to do basic painting and cleaning with perhaps new window coverings and lighting. On the other hand, you may need to do a complete fix-up including new appliances, cabinets, countertops, flooring, and so on using the very best materials (as would be the case with million-dollar-plus homes). The difference in cost, as noted earlier, can be enormous.

So, what should you do?

As indicated when we started this chapter, if you're going to sell, you don't want to fix anything that isn't broken. If the current kitchen is up to neighborhood norms, is clean, with nothing broken, *do nothing* except clean and paint.

 KEY CONCEPT *Sometimes the best course of action is to take no action.*

On the other hand, there may be things that are broken (and I include obsolescence under the heading of broken items). If it's broken, it needs to be fixed. Let's consider each item usually found in the kitchen.

Kitchen Stove/Oven—Cost: $350 to $5,000

If the stove is relatively new and in good working order, all that's needed may be a thorough cleaning, which can cost $50 from a maid service. If the stove doesn't work, it has to be fixed. However, often it's easier and cheaper to buy new than to fix. For example, you can often buy a complete new electric range for the cost of fixing two broken burners. On the other hand, if it's an expensive stove that adds value to the home, fixing it may be more cost effective.

As always, check out the competition. What kind of stoves are in their kitchens? How does yours compare? Your stove should be comparable to what the competition offers. If you put in a more expensive and higher quality stove, you're probably wasting money. Put in a lesser quality stove and it will detract when the buyers compare your home with competitors'.

A word of caution: don't try to substitute a different type of stove/oven for what you have. If you have electric, stay with it. If you have gas, go with that. The cost of dragging either a 220-volt line or a gas line where none exist can exceed the cost of the appliance.

Kitchen Countertop—Cost: $1,200 to $20,000 installed

You should be aware that some people adjust the value of a home based entirely on the countertop found in the kitchen. The reason is that prices vary enormously for countertops, and many buyers figure that how much you spend here indicates how much you've spent elsewhere. The quality of the material used in the countertop is often seen as a marker against which all the other items in the house can be measured. If you're going to scrimp anywhere, *do not* scrimp on a countertop.

I was recently involved in the sale of a nearly new apartment building. Having followed the construction from the time the foundation was laid, I was well aware that only the cheapest of materials and least costly workmanship were used. However, when the apartments were being finished off, the contractor/owner made sure that each kitchen had a small granite countertop. This was by far the most costly and best quality item used in the apartments.

When I asked the contractor/owner why he used granite, he told me that granite has become the de facto standard of fine quality in residential kitchens. (That's not to say that it's the most expensive countertop; it's not, although it is more expensive than many other types of material.) What's more important, he said, is that it is universally recognized as being part of a quality home. People in general have a reaction something like, "Wow, it's got a granite countertop—it must be a quality residence."

The contractor/owner told me, "I'll get $100 a month more rent for the units because of the granite. That means each unit is worth about $15,000 more when I sell. It's certainly worth the few thousand it cost to put in." When he rented up he was right, and he was right when he later sold.

This is not to say that you must use granite for your kitchen countertop, although you could certainly do worse. It's just to say that whatever you use for a countertop is very important to how a buyer sees your home.

First determine the condition of the existing countertop. Older homes generally have tile countertops. There's nothing wrong with this, if the tile isn't broken and isn't an unappealing color, and if the grout is clean. On the other hand, if there are broken tiles; it's pink, lavender, or some other nonneutral color; and the grout is filthy (as is usually the case with old tile), you should consider putting in something new. You probably could replace the old countertop with new inexpensive tile for as little as $2,500, if the area isn't too big. If you use expensive foreign tiles, the price could quadruple. What's interesting is that for not much more, you can put in an inexpensive granite countertop with a tile splash board.

On the other hand, your existing countertop may not be tile. It could be a laminate such as Formica®, or stone, or some synthetic material such as Corian®. Once again, take a close look at its condition. If it's not discolored, or broken, or burned, or otherwise damaged, then consider whether it's obsolete. Does it look old-fashioned and, as a result, make the house look that way?

Not sure? Again, check out other homes in the neighborhood and see what their countertops are like. Also, spend a few minutes at the kitchen department in stores such as Lowe's and Home Depot. You'll quickly see what works and what doesn't.

Your existing countertop meets neighborhood norms and is modern? It's not broken? Then simply clean it and leave it alone.

For a typical kitchen here are some prices for countertops made of the most common materials* (using medium-quality grade):

---

* Note: There are hundreds of types of materials that can be used for a countertop; check with a good cabinet/countertop store. I've only listed a few.

Countertop Costs

- Granite $3,500 to $7,000
- Synthetic granite $3,000 to $5,000
- Soapstone $3,500 to $10,000
- Tile $2,500 to $5,000
- Laminate $1,200 to $3,000
- Cement (laid in place) $7,000+

Kitchen Cabinets—Cost: $3,500 to $25,000 installed*

Because of the high replacement cost, my suggestion is that you try to get by with the existing cabinets, unless they are beyond repair. An exception to this is when using a heavy material, such as granite, that requires a sturdy, level base. Old cabinets may not be capable of supporting a granite or other heavy countertop. To save the old cabinets, you may want to consider a different countertop option such as laminate. (Tile also needs a sturdy base, but if the old cabinets can be strengthened sufficiently, a bed of concrete sometimes can be floated on top and the tile laid on that.)

Things to look for in old cabinets are cracks, broken hinges, sagging doors, open grain in the wood (usually caused by water damage), and, most important, an old-fashioned appearance that lacks modern styling. Keep in mind that a lot can be done with sanding, paint, and stain. However, after a point it simply becomes cheaper and easier to replace old cabinets than to attempt to fix them.

In some cases it is possible to reface the existing, old cabinets. Contractors are available to do this (use keyword "cabinet refacing" on the Internet). Typically, they use the old cabinets and replace the doors. Be aware, however, that the price is often almost as much as for entirely replacing the cabinets with inexpensive new ones.

---

* The cost is determined by the number of cabinets needed and the quality selected.

There are dozens of major cabinet manufacturers in this country, and almost all of them offer a range of lines from inexpensive to costly. I've used the inexpensive lines of quality manufacturers to replace cabinets in kitchens. The result is often at the low end of the price range—$3,500 to $5,000—yet the results are strikingly good looking. It's something to consider.

 KEY CONCEPT *If you plan to replace the countertop with expensive materials, it usually makes sense to also replace the cabinets at the same time.*

Most old cabinets can be painted. (Use oil-based paints to cover cabinets that have been stained.) If you use a high-quality gloss paint, the result can be strikingly good looking. The cost, however, is typically $2,000 to $3,000 to have a professional do the work. And keep in mind it doesn't pay to do this if the cabinets are old-fashioned in design (obsolete) or unsturdy.

Kitchen Sink, Faucets—Cost: $250 to $3,500 plus installation

If you're going to put in a new countertop, by all means put in a new sink and faucets. Chances are you won't have a choice because the old sink and faucet will probably be damaged in the demolition process.

Today, stainless steel seems to be the most fashionable type of sink (to match other appliances in the kitchen). But fashions change and tomorrow color porcelain may be back or there may be a switch to glass. Once again, check with your neighborhood competition. Don't overdo it. If all the competing homes have porcelain sinks, go with that. Here are some typical prices for kitchen sinks and faucet assemblies:

Kitchen Sinks and Faucet Assemblies

- Stainless $150 to $2,500*

- Porcelain $75 to $250

- Ceramic $350 to $2,000

- Glass $1,000 to $5,000

- Synthetic $75 to $150 (not usually recommend for kitchens)

- Faucet assemblies $50 to $2,500 (often a brand name assembly for around $200 will look elegant for a year or more)

Kitchen: Other Appliances

Dish Washer—Cost: $250 to $2,500 plus installation. If the existing washer doesn't work, has a rusty/stained front, or if you're putting in a new countertop and cabinets, replace it. If not, clean it and go with it.

If you're doing a minimum kitchen makeover, you can get a washer that looks OK and works adequately for $250. However, most buyers can spot bottom-of-the-line appliances. So, for another $250 you can get a dishwasher that looks modern and offers better visual value. (It will cost you approaching $1,000 to get one that offers true sound reduction, stainless steel tub, and digital features throughout; only worth it if you're doing a high-cost kitchen makeover.)

Kitchen Garbage Disposal—Cost: $75 to $200 plus installation. Replace if the old one doesn't work, or if you're putting in a new sink. The minimum horsepower to be effective is 3/4 hp. You

---

* Note: Inexpensive stainless steel sinks are often of thinner gauge metal and show water stains. Many buyers are aware of this, so if you can't buy a better quality stainless sink (typically starting at around $500), it might be better to use another material.

can get this for only about $35 more, so it's worth it not to have to worry about the disposal jamming when a potential buyer comes by and tries it out.

Kitchen Garbage Compactor—Cost: $200 to $1,000 plus installation. Not expected except in top-quality kitchens, so don't waste your money here, unless it's required by neighborhood norms.

Kitchen Microwave Oven Hood—Cost: $250 to $1,000 plus installation. Again, not expected by most buyers, so don't waste your money on it. If you're replacing countertop and cabinets, you can get a conventional oven hood for under $100, or you may be able to clean and reuse the old one.

Kitchen Floor—Cost: $600 to $8,500 installed

Never underestimate the importance of flooring, especially in a kitchen. I was recently in a home where the countertop, cabinets, and appliances were modern, clean, and good looking. The floor, however, was a yellow square linoleum print. Its color didn't match the rest of the room, its pattern was abrasive, and it simply looked cheap. The agent mentioned in confidence that she was convinced the kitchen floor was turning off buyers. She said she had tried to get the sellers to put in a new floor, but they refused, saying they liked the existing color, and besides, they didn't want to spend any more fix-up money.

Mistake. Don't exclude the floor when you fix up the kitchen. The floor is a huge part of the area of the kitchen. It's hard to miss when you walk in. And if it looks bad, the whole curb appeal of the room can be turned negative.

If the existing kitchen floor is cracked, broken, torn, worn, or simply looks bad or outdated, replace it. Today you can get amazingly good-looking linoleum floors that cost in the hundreds, not the thousands, of dollars. These often mimic the most costly materials such as marble, stone, and tile.

Of course, for a more elegant approach you can go with tile, wood (natural or manufactured), or stone, although cost jumps up enormously. Be sure to check the neighborhood norms to see what's justified in your kitchen.

Beware of overspending on the kitchen floor; it's easy to do. Many sellers say they've always wanted a wood floor or a tile floor in the kitchen and pop for it as part of a kitchen makeover. Mistake. You're not going to be living in the home—you're going to be selling it! Don't put in a better floor than is normal for your neighborhood. You may end up being proud of the appearance, but the sales price won't justify the cost.

Kitchen Ceiling—Cost: $150 to $5,000 installed (or painted)

This is truly a case where if it isn't broken, don't fix it. In many modern homes there are dropped ceilings in the kitchen with recessed lighting and even exotic wood or synthetic panels. They look great. But, unless your home is in the multi-million-dollar range, it probably won't pay to do anything more to the ceiling than to paint it and let it go. Quite frankly, rarely will a seller be justified in putting in a new kitchen ceiling.

Of course, there are always exceptions. If all the neighboring homes have updated kitchen ceilings, if the existing ceiling is cracked, too low, severely unattractive, or otherwise defective, you'll have to pop for the money to fix it.

Bathroom Fix
Total Cost: $1,500 to $40,000 Installed

As with a kitchen, the cost depends on the quality of materials chosen. And also, as with the kitchen, how much you do depends on how bad the existing bathrooms are and how they differ from neighborhood norms.

Your first step, however, should be to identify the importance of the bathroom with which you're dealing. There are four areas where bathrooms are found in homes:

- The master bath (off the master bedroom); the most important for buyers.
- The guest bath (usually found near the living areas off a hallway); the second most important.
- The secondary bathroom (found off other bedrooms); of nominal importance to buyers.
- The utility bathroom (usually found near the back door); of little to no importance to buyers.

Master Bathroom

In today's homes, this is a critical feature secondary only to the kitchen in importance to most buyers. If you have a large home with four bathrooms, the other three will pale in significance when compared with this one. If you have an elegant master bathroom, most buyers will overlook sometimes significant defects in the other baths. If you're going to do work on only one bathroom, make this the one.

But don't overdo it. I saw a seller who had lived in her home for six years with a bath/shower combination in the master bathroom. However, she always wanted a separate shower stall. So, when she decided to sell, the first thing she did was hire a contractor to put in a separate shower stall. The cost was more than $20,000.

Because the house was otherwise in excellent shape and well staged, it sold almost immediately. But the price probably wasn't even $1,000 more than she would have gotten if she had simply left the bathroom alone with the bath/shower combination.

KEY CONCEPT *Don't waste your money on things that don't need to be done and that won't bring a high return on the cost.*

Yes, buyers definitely liked the idea of a separate shower. But, no, they weren't going to pay extra for it. And because she sold soon after the improvement, she benefited little from it herself. Of course, the worst part was spending that money and not recouping it.

Buyers like big bathrooms, but if you have a small bathroom, my suggestion is that you think twice before enlarging it. Occasionally making a bathroom bigger is an easy fix, as when you can convert a nearby closet to bathroom space. In most homes, however, it requires adding on (discussed later), which is almost always the kiss of death for fixes.

Guest Bathroom

This is the next most important bathroom, because it's what guests of the buyers will see. Work here will also pay off, but only about half as well as for a master bathroom.

Secondary Bathroom(s)

If your home should have more than two bathrooms, buyers will typically overlook obsolescence and even some defects here. However, the room should be staged properly—clean, well painted, and without odors.

Utility Bathroom

Almost anything goes here. Don't waste time and money on this bathroom. Just clean it, remove clutter (make sure there aren't any dirty towels or waste around), and move on. The exception, of course, is if there's something seriously broken like a cracked sink or toilet. Such things must be fixed.

Bathroom Countertop—Cost: $100 to $4,000 installed

As with the kitchen, this is usually the first thing that buyers look at in a bathroom. They tend to judge the quality of the bathroom overall by the quality of the countertop.

If the countertop is, for example, Corian (cost: $1,200+) or a similar material, they will assume the bathroom is upgraded. If the countertop is synthetic marble (cost: $100), they'll likely think it's not.

Money spent on the bathroom countertop usually pays off. However, whereas with a kitchen, stone is the gold standard, with bathrooms, tile (cost: $500 to $1,500) is often preferred. (People have long expected to see good-quality tile in bathrooms.) This is particularly the case if you select a quality sink(s) to go with it.

Most bathrooms in older homes are either tile or synthetic marble. If the countertop is in good shape (no cracked tiles and dirt in the grout, no burns or defects in the marble), you're probably best off leaving well enough alone. Unless the neighbors have all upgraded, let it go with a good cleaning. On the other hand, if the countertop looks bad, you should seriously consider replacing it.

Bathroom Sink (Basin)—Cost: $50 to $2,000 plus installation

In case you haven't noticed, there's been a revolution in bathroom sinks. Today they are made of glass, bronze, and a host of other manufactured materials. Some of the nicest are free standing, sitting on top of the countertop. They add an unmistakable touch of elegance.

While you can easily get a porcelain-covered metal sink for $50, it will look cheap. On the other hand, for a couple of hundred bucks, you can get a ceramic sink ($100 to $250). And if the neighborhood warrants it, put in one of the more modern, free-standing sinks (around $400 to $2,000). Because the countertop area in a bathroom is so small, the quality of the sink is very important.

Bathroom Faucets—Cost: $50 to $1,500 plus installation

It should go without saying that all the bathroom fixtures should *match*. Nothing says cheap like mismatched faucets handles or different types of faucets on the shower, tub, and sink. If they're mismatched, replace them all. (You can't easily find matches for old faucets.)

If you add a new countertop and sink, add a faucet of equal quality. But be aware that good bathroom faucets can easily cost $500 or more. However, again, if the faucet and sink are of unequal quality, it says cheap. (It's sort of like a man wearing a suit with mismatched jacket and pants.)

Fixtures (Lights, Mirror, Towel Rack)—Cost: $50 to $1,500 plus installation

Unless the existing fixtures are in perfect condition, simply replace them. (Old fixtures typically have tarnish, peeling, stains, or other defects.) You can usually get a spectacular mirror for around $100 at Lowe's or Home Depot. Stylish, sparkling new towel racks, paper holder, and clothes hooks are readily available in the $50 (apiece) range for a set. Good-looking lighting fixtures can be purchased for under $100 (plus, of course, installation).

Of course, if you go with elegant fixtures, the price jumps up considerably. Most times, however, this is unnecessary. Remember, you don't want to overdo it.

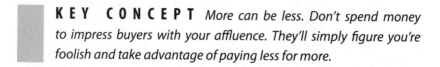

KEY CONCEPT *More can be less. Don't spend money to impress buyers with your affluence. They'll simply figure you're foolish and take advantage of paying less for more.*

Bathroom Floor—Cost: $300 to $2,500 installed

There's nothing wrong with an inexpensive linoleum floor in a bathroom—as long as that's what all the competing homes have.

However, today most modern homes have (sometimes) expensive tile floors in the bathroom, such as travertine, or they may even use natural stone. Here, it's a case of "keeping up with the Joneses." If their bathroom floor has it, then it will look definitely cheap if yours doesn't. It will set your home apart as not worthy of an offer in the high range.

However, even if competing homes have 2-foot-square travertine pieces, you don't need to use such an expensive tile. You can use inexpensive small 6-inch by 6-inch tiles and have an acceptable appearance. If you do tile your floor, however, be sure that the tile comes up the wall a bit in a splash guard. The cost can be under $600 for common tiles.

Bathroom Tub/Shower—Cost: $250 to 6,000 installed

If your home has a separate tub and shower in the master bath and elsewhere, fine. If it doesn't, don't try adding it. Unless you're in the million-dollar-plus range, it won't be worth the cost.

If it's a tile shower, be sure the tiles are not cracked and the grout is clean. If it's just the grout, it can be cleaned in a shower. If it's a few cracked tiles, sometimes they can be replaced with a different color accent tiles. (Matching old tiles is usually impossible.)

If you must replace a shower enclosure, consider using one of the new plastic enclosures that can be inset. They are available at most large hardware stores, can be installed by almost anyone, and only cost a few hundred dollars. If they won't work, then consider an inexpensive tile job. But, if you do the shower, do the floor and possibly the countertop at the same time with the same material.

Most older tubs are just fine with a bit of cleanser and elbow grease. If they are the old porcelain tub type, however, they may have cracks and chips. This is an unsightly defect and should be fixed. My experience with "painting" over chips with porcelain paint has not been good. Even when it works, it looks like a cheap fix. Instead, consider having the tub reporcenalized. People who do this are readily available. They come in, and in a day, without moving the tub, it looks like brand new . . . for only a few hundred dollars. Check with your local building supply store or plumber for recommendations.

If you have a whirlpool tub, be sure it works, doesn't leak, and all the outlets are clean. (They tend to get stained over time from calcium and other deposits in the water.) A building supply store will offer products that help remove the stains when applied with a bit of elbow grease. (I've not found one that's particularly better than another.)

Bathroom Fan—Cost: $25 to $45

These are typically installed in bathrooms that don't have windows. They may go on when the light is turned on, or they may have a separate switch. They rarely stop working, but over time often develop a loud rattle. If yours makes noise, replace it. It's a cheap item to fix, and it will prevent buyers from gritting their teeth at the noise when they throw the switch.

Today's fans are rated in "sones" or noise levels. A sone of 5 is considered noisy; 2 is considered quiet. Get a quiet fan so that when a buyer turns it on, it doesn't make him or her cringe at the noise.

Entry Fix
Cost: $25 to $5,000

Rather than cover each room in the house separately from now on, we'll discuss general issues such as carpeting, lighting, plumbing, and so on, with one exception. The entry.

Every home has an entry, even it doesn't know it. The entry is where the buyer first steps when he or she enters your home. It can be an elegant room with chandelier, tile flooring, papered walls, and magnificent views. Or it can be simply a piece of wood flooring or carpeting undistinguished from the rest of the room.

Regardless, think of curb appeal once more. It's the first impression. It's the initial impression the inside of your home makes on the buyer. Therefore, I suggest that if you have an acceptable entry in which nothing is broken, stained, or detracting, at the least make it sparklingly clean, paint it, scrub the floors, and do whatever else it takes to clean it up. On the other hand, if there are defects in the entry, fix them. Fix cracked tile (or put in a new floor), fix the chandelier or get a better one, paint or stain handrails, and so on.

Finally, if your home doesn't have a formal entry, make one. (Even if the norm in your neighborhood is to have no entry!) This is an exception to the rule about norms because it will make your home stand out from the rest for a nominal cost.

It's simple to create an entry. Just make the flooring different in back of the front door. If your home has wall-to-wall carpeting, a 4-foot by 6-foot slab of tile (a couple hundred dollars installed) behind the front door makes an acceptable entry. Put a nice mat down and it gives buyers a place to stamp their feet clean when they enter.

Yes, adding a new entry may take away a few square feet of living space. But, it sets the entrance off from the rest of the home and makes for a much better "curb appeal" when entering the home. It also suggests a richer interior.

Where possible, hang a light over the entry. It makes it brighter and more cheery. Adding a coat tree to hang coats on completes the work.

Of course, if you already have an entry, make it look its best.

Flooring Fix
Cost: $3,000 to $15,000 Installed for the Whole House

People tend to look down when they walk, and buyers are no exception. Thus, the part of your home that's likely to get the most scrutiny, perhaps inadvertently, is your flooring, making this is another area where special attention is needed.

If you have word flooring, is it scratched, marked, chipped, stained, or otherwise defective? If it is, do what it takes to get it fixed. These can range from a simple polishing to sanding and restaining.

Do you have wall-to-wall carpeting? Most homes do. Check it thoroughly for:

- Dirt
- Stains
- Marks
- Rips and tears
- Excessive wear (in heavily trafficked areas)
- Color (purple is out; neutral light brown is in)

All of these points constitute defects that need fixing. The first three might be fixable by a thorough cleaning. You won't know, however, until you try. Expect to pay several hundred dollars to have the whole house carpeting cleaned.

If the cleaning doesn't remove the dirt, stains, and marks, or if you have rips, tears, and excessive wear, consider replacing the carpet. For a home of 2,000 square feet with roughly 1,600 square feet of carpeting, you can get a whole house replacement of inexpensive carpeting for around $3,500 installed. (When buying new carpeting, be sure to get a neutral color; this is discussed in great detail in Chapter 7.)

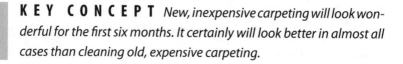

KEY CONCEPT *New, inexpensive carpeting will look wonderful for the first six months. It certainly will look better in almost all cases than cleaning old, expensive carpeting.*

Don't try to "get by" with damaged carpeting. If it doesn't clean up well, bite the bullet and get it replaced. You'll almost certainly get a quicker sale for more money.

Heating/Cooling System
Cost: $100 to $10,000 Installed

This is a no-brainer. If it works, don't fix it. If it's broken, fix it.

If you have to fix it, go for the least expensive fix possible. Remember, you're not going to live in the home long enough to recoup the costs of an expensive fix or a complete replacement. The new owners will get those benefits. Most heating/cooling systems can be fixed and brought up to working order for a fraction of the cost of replacement. Do that.

The only exception *might* be if the existing heating/cooling system is inadequate, in other words, if a system that's too small was put in. If that's the case, you might have to replace with a newer system, simply to make the house salable. This is particularly the case where the house is located in an area of extreme temperatures.

Electrical System Fix
Cost: $25 to $10,000 Installed*

Usually, but not always, a no-brainer. If there are a few broken outlets and switches, have them fixed. That's usually it.

Of course, there are always exceptions, particularly if you have an older home. Depending on the age of the property and how it was wired, the electrical system may be inadequate for today's modern needs. Plug in a hair dryer, use the toaster, and turn on the clothes dryer all at the same time, and fuses may blow.

This could be not only an inconvenience but also a safety issue. You may need to have the home rewired to make it usable in the modern world. The cost could be anywhere from $4,000 to $10,000, depending on how many walls need to be knocked out and repaired in the process. You might have to pop for the cost in order to sell a safe home.

---

* Note: Have all electrical work done professionally. That helps avoid liability for you if something bad happens after you sell.

Here are some other serious electrical issues that you may need to address before you sell your property:

Electrical Concerns Usually Found in Older Homes

- *Ground wire missing throughout home* (the third bare or green wire in most circuits): Fix requires complete rewiring of home; cost: $7,000+.

- *No ground fault interrupter plugs in kitchen and bath:* A safety issue that can usually be remedied with new GFI plugs, but it could require rewiring; cost: $10 per plug.

- *Missing or damaged insulation on wires:* Typical of very old homes and requires rewiring; cost: $7,000+.

- *Circuit breaker panel too small:* Modern panels are 200 amps and higher. Older and middle-aged homes (30 to 60 years old) may have smaller panels that are inadequate (circuits always blowing). Requires installing new panel; cost: as much as $1,000+.

- *Disconnected or never-connected circuits:* Found even in new homes and usually requires rewiring the circuit; cost: $350+.

Plumbing (Potable Water) Fix
Total Cost: $100 to $10,000 Installed

It all depends on what's wrong. At the least, it will simply be a worn-out washer on a faucet that you can fix yourself for 50 cents. At worst it will be corroded and leaking pipes (typically galvanized) that require a whole house replacement costing as much as $10,000 or more.

You can tell if a faucet is leaking by the drip. You can tell if the pipes are leaking by sudden water appearing in unexpected places (such as dripping from the ceiling or walls or bubbling up from the floors).

For homes with galvanized pipe, the lifespan of the pipe usually depends on two things—the corrosive elements in the water and the electrostatic condition of the soil. Most plumbers will tell you that if you get one leak in galvanized pipe, you just fix it and hope for the best. If you get two, chances are the pipe throughout the house is like Swiss cheese (filled with holes ready to burst) and it's time to repipe the whole place.

Many sellers with homes containing leaking galvanized pipe will simply fix the leaks as they occur using pressure pads (cost: about $10 plus installation) and then just disclose the problem to buyers. Because this is one of those things that can't be seen, often buyers will simply accept the disclosures and move on. However, like a leaking roof, eventually someone will have to repipe the house.

Today most homes use either or both copper and PVC plumbing. It tends to never leak or need replacement.

Water Heater—Cost: $250 to $750 installed

If the water heater doesn't leak, don't fix it. Period.

Of course, the water heater may be too small for the house. If that's the case, out of the generosity of your heart, you can install a newer, bigger one. But, don't expect to recoup a penny of your expense.

If the water heater leaks, replace it. You can't normally fix a leaking water heater.

Wastewater System—Cost: $100 to $5,000

Usually, the only thing to go wrong with the drains is that they get plugged. Call a plumber to root them out ($100 to $150) and things usually work fine again . . . until the next time.

Things get more serious when trees plug and break the drain lines (a real possibility with older homes using clay or cast iron pipe instead of black PVC). This can require digging up the drain (usually the main line) and replacing it. Expect to spend $1,200 to $5,000.

Leaking drains (usually found in kitchens and bathrooms) have become an enormous problem. It's not that they're difficult to fix—a plumber can usually do that job in less than an hour, so your charge should be under $100. It's that the leak tends to produce black mold.

Today, black mold is the biggest taboo in home selling. Most buyers simply won't even consider a home with black mold. If you have it because of leaky pipes, after you fix the pipes, you'll have to have the mold removed. This could include removing wall boards, insulation, cabinets, and so on, by men in space suits. The cost can be phenomenal, and each case is on its own in terms of price.

Of course, you can do the work yourself for a fraction of the cost. But, there are health risks. And buyers may not accept your work.

KEY CONCEPT *You should disclose to buyers any black mold found in the home and how it was removed. Black mold is a fungus associated with allergies and, in some cases, with illness and even death. It occurs when there is moisture, often occurring from plumbing leaks. Remediation usually requires professional assistance and is expensive. Buyers today are very anxious about black mold in a home, and failure to disclose it could result in a lawsuit after the sale. The buyers could demand damages, even insist that you rescind the contract and take the home back! It's not something to play games with. Get rid of any black mold, properly.*

Basement
Cost: $25 to $10,000 Installed*

There are a variety of problems that can be associated with a basement. How you fix these should be determined by their sever-

---

* Note: We're not including the cost to convert a basement from storage to living space. See the discussion on home additions later.

ity and by what the basement is used for. If the basement is simply an area where a heater is located and where excess items are stored, you can probably get away with minimal correction work. On the other hand, if the basement is used as living space, then more severe remedial work may be required.

Typical Problems with Basements and Fixes

- *Structural cracks:* A thorough fix could require rebuilding the foundation or at the least adding supports. Consult with a structural and soils engineer. A temporary fix is filling the cracks and painting over. Caution: Don't attempt to *hide* cracks from buyers by cosmetically sealing. Disclose all cracks to reduce your liability. Cost: $100 (for paint and sealer) to $75,000+ to replace foundation

- *Water seepage:* Symptoms include stains on the walls and floor as well as dampness. Determine the cause and eliminate it. French drains around the perimeter of the home and even a sump pump may be needed. Cost: $250 to $2,500

- *Warping:* Caused by moisture affecting paneling. Replace panels and remove moisture as noted earlier.

- *Black mold:* Caused by moisture. Remove moisture as noted earlier. Hire a pest and termite company to eradicate the mold. Cost: $2,000 to $10,000+

- *Odor:* Caused by moisture. Remove moisture as noted earlier. Check for mold. Remove insulation and paneling that harbors odor. Use a dehumidifier and odor covering strips. $10 to $500

Drainage
Cost: $250 to $5,000 Installed

Very often severe problems in homes can be corrected by simple drainage fixes. For example, cracked foundations, slabs, and basements are often caused by standing water under the house. Leaning fences, cracks in walls and ceilings (inside and out), and puddling in the yard can also be the result of poor drainage.

The basic concept with drainage for all homes is that water must be led away from the structure. In most cases, this means that the water is directed around the house and out to the street. In homes that are below street level, it is usually directed away, toward the back of the property.

If the land was properly graded, the simplest fix usually involves clearing trash and accumulated debris and dirt from the side yards. This will allow water to move around the house and to the street.

Where the lot was not properly graded, new grading may be necessary. Drains may also be employed to direct the water from the back, around the sides, and to the street. (French drains are buried about a foot below soil level and have holes in the pipes so that water will fill them and then flow away—a very effective means of drainage. These drains can usually be installed in a conventional lot for a few thousand dollars.)

In areas where there isn't sufficient slope for drains, a sump pump may be needed to catch standing water and then pump it out to the street (cost: $500 to $1,500 installed).

Roof gutters are an important part of any drainage system. They direct water from the roof through downspouts and away from the house.

Once the water is away from the house, new damage to foundations and other areas is usually eliminated and existing problems can be quickly, and often inexpensively, stabilized.

Don't attempt to fix the apparent problem (cracks, movement, mold, etc.) until the cause—poor drainage—has been eliminated. If you do, you'll have wasted your efforts.

Attic
Cost: $500 to $7,500 Installed*

As with the basement, it all depends on what the attic is used for. If your home's attic is not used to live in, but instead is empty or used to as a storage space, only a minimal fix may be needed. On the other hand, if the attic is used as living space, then any problem will need to be fully corrected.

Typical Problems with Attics and Fixes

- *Water stains:* Caused by roof leaks. Fix the roof (see later discussion) and paint over the stains. Any damaged wood should also be replaced. Cost: $200 to $1,500 installed

- *Black mold:* Caused by moisture. Primarily from roof leaks, but also from moisture rising through ceiling from below. Install a moisture barrier and use a dehumidifier. Cost: $2,000 to $10,000+ professionally done

- *Warping:* Again, a moisture problem, possibly from moisture through ceiling above. Install a moisture barrier and use a dehumidifier—cost $250 to $1,000.

- *Odors:* Either from moisture or from the living areas below. Keep door to attic closed, use dehumidifier and air freshener strips. Cost: $10 to $150

Roof
Cost: $500 to $40,000

The rule here is most definitely, if it isn't broken, don't fix it. If it is broken, try your best to have it repaired. Consider replacing a roof only as a last resort. The reason, of course, is the enormous cost of roof replacement. As a worst-case scenario, have the roof at

---

* Note: We're not including the cost to convert an attic from storage to living space. Check home addition discussion later.

least temporarily fixed, then disclose the roof's bad condition and offer to split the cost with a buyer. (If you don't have it at least temporarily fixed, the buyers will argue that you're selling a home they can't even move into.)

Have a good roofer check your roof. This often can be done by standing across the street and examining the roof through binoculars. Also, look up at the roof from the attic during a sunny day to see if light comes through, indicating leaks. Having someone use a hose to spray water, especially on metal flashing, can also reveal leaks.

Many leaks are caused by a deterioration of sealing materials around chimney and vent flashing. These types of leaks can often quickly be resealed by a roofer, eliminating the problem (cost: $250+). In other cases, a leaking roof can be repaired. In the case of wooden shingles, typically a few have blown off, exposing the waterproofing material underneath, which has then torn. A fix can be accomplished by replacing the waterproofing material where damaged and adding new wood shingles (cost: $150 to $1,000+). The same sort of repair can be accomplished with tile roofs. However, because tile is fragile and removing, storing, and then replacing after the underlayment has been replaced is difficult, the cost can be higher (cost: $500 to $2,500+). Metal roof repairs can be more difficult because entire sheets may need to be replaced. Cement and other synthetic roofs likewise may require special treatment.

Here is a summary of roofing problems and fixes:

Typical Roof Fixes

- *Wood shingle:* Replace missing shingles and underlayment. May require repairs at many different locations. Fixing cost: $100 to $1,500+ (Note: Local building codes may require conversion to a nonflammable roof.)

- *Composition shingle* (Fiberglass, asphalt, etc.—one of the least expensive roofs): Can be fixed *if* you can find the exact material originally used. (Sometimes leftovers are stored in the garage or basement.) If the roofing material has curled at the edges (as happens in hot climates such as in the Southwest), a whole roof replacement may be needed. Cost to fix: $3,000 to $5,000+

- *Ceramic tile:* Very costly to replace or repair. Must be done by professionals to avoid breaking tiles. Cost: $300 to as much as $40,000+ to replace

- *Metal:* Usually lasts forever but is subject to dents and rips from branches falling on it. May be able to replace a single panel or two. Cost to fix: $500+

- *Cement shingle:** Usually lasts a lifetime. Subject to breaking, just like tile. Must be replaced and repaired professionally—$300 to $10,000+.

Caution: If you replace a roof, don't do so with a less expensive material than is normal for the neighborhood, or you'll degrade the home's value.

K E Y   C O N C E P T   *If the roof needs replacing, you should consider offering the buyers a credit toward part of the cost, rather than replacing it yourself. This allows the buyer to choose the type of roof he or she wants. It also means that the buyer will pay a part of the cost, instead of you paying the entire burden. Most buyers are amenable to such an offer on big-ticket items.*

---

* Cement shingles are a relatively new product and are used because of their long lifespan, fireproof qualities, and good looks. They often replace wood or composition roofs. However, they are much heavier, and if the original roof is not structurally strengthened, can cause cracking, buckling and other serious problems in the house. If this occurs, you may need to contact the roofer who replaced the original roof with cement tiles. (Sometimes litigation is necessary to get the problem corrected.) It will be difficult to sell a home that is buckling under the weight of a too heavy roof—a fix is almost always needed.

Add-On Fixes
Cost: $5,000+

First ask yourself, why would you want to add onto a home that you're about to sell?

The reason that people usually give for adding on rooms is that the home is too small. You need more space for yourself and your family.

A good reason, for the buyer of your home to add on, not you!

The only time it even remotely makes sense to add on is when your home is too small for the neighborhood norms. Your house has only one bathroom, and all the other homes that are in competition with it have two or more. Adding on a bathroom can make sense.

Your home only has one or two bedrooms. All the competitors have two or three. Adding on can make sense.

Your home doesn't have a garage, yet every other home in the neighborhood does. Constructing a garage can add real value (particularly if you're in an area with severe winter weather where keeping a car in the garage is almost a necessity).

With these exceptions, adding on space will usually only add cost to your home, not commensurate value. For every dollar you pay for the addition, chances are you'll get 40 cents or less back when you sell.

On the other hand, if you're planning to sell your home three years or more from now, by all means consider adding on. You'll benefit from the addition by using it yourself, and the cost-to-value ratio won't matter so much.

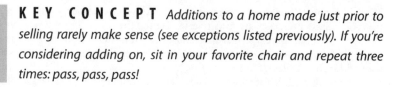

K E Y   C O N C E P T *Additions to a home made just prior to selling rarely make sense (see exceptions listed previously). If you're considering adding on, sit in your favorite chair and repeat three times: pass, pass, pass!*

Additions Other Than Space
Cost: $250++

You may want to add a skylight to a living area that's always dark. This can be done for between $250 and $1,000 (including installation) and may so much improve and brighten your home that you'll get every dime back.

Adding a deck can also make sense, particularly if there's a view. The cost can be under $2,500 for a moderately sized one if you do the work yourself or $10,000+ installed using top-grade materials.

Conversions can also make sense. For example, you want to increase the size of your master bedroom. And it just so happens that right next to it is a large walk-in closet from a different bedroom. Converting the walk-in closet from the other bedroom to more space for your master bedroom can also make sense. (You could always add an armoire to the bedroom you took the closet from.)

Beware of converting bedrooms to other uses. For example, converting a 3-bedroom home to two bedrooms and using that lost bedroom to make a bigger master bedroom rarely makes sense. Usually a 3-bedroom home is considered a minimum size. (On the other hand, converting a 5-bedroom home to four using the lost bedroom to increase the master's size could make sense—*if* the master bedroom was so small as to deter from the value of the home.)

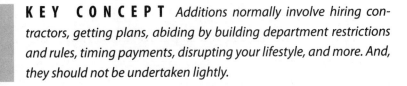

K E Y   C O N C E P T *Additions normally involve hiring contractors, getting plans, abiding by building department restrictions and rules, timing payments, disrupting your lifestyle, and more. And, they should not be undertaken lightly.*

Backyard Fix
Cost: $100 to $10,000+ Installed

A wonderful backyard with lawns, shrubs, pool, fountains, patio, gazebo, and so on, will definitely help sell a home. The trouble is it won't sell it for anywhere near the price it costs to put that backyard in.

As a result, I suggest you think of the minimal amount of fixing when it comes to your backyard. First, ask yourself, "Is it broken?"

Bare dirt and weeds is considered broken. It detracts from the home. However, simply adding a lawn, a few flower beds, and some lawn chairs can transform that broken yard into one that, at the least, won't detract from the sale. Add a small deck (concrete or wood), and you have your minimal backyard. The cost can be a few thousand dollars or less.

My suggestion is, that's all you do. *Don't* fix the backyard just prior to sale by putting in any of the following:

- Pool or spa (unless you're in an area of multi-million-dollar homes where every house has them). *A pool usually has the worst cost-to-value ratio of any single thing you can add to a home.*

- Large deck (although a small one is usually worthwhile).

- Gazebo or patio cover—simply unnecessary for a sale.

- Extensive gardens—it's overkill; simple flower beds, lawn, and elementary shrubs will do.

- Fish pond—don't bother, for the same reasons as those given for a pool.

- Children's play equipment (unless you want to gift it to the buyers, who may ask you to pay to haul it away if they don't have children).

Pool/Spa Equipment
Cost: $250 to $5,000

If you have a pool or spa, you're going to also have the equipment that's needed to run it. Most basically this includes a filter, pump, and heater. You could additionally have a pump to produce air in the spa, a secondary pump for additional water pressure in the spa, a robot to clean the pool, and so on.

If any of this equipment is broken, fix it. The buyers will assume it's all in working condition and will almost certainly make that a condition of sale. If it's broken, they'll automatically assume it needs to be replaced, not fixed. And that's far more expensive.

So save yourself a headache and additional expense by fixing any broken equipment early on. Pumps (around $300–$600) usually should be replaced rather than repaired (repairing means they could go out again, while the house is being shown). Heaters can usually be fixed. If they can't, an inexpensive heater can easily cost $1,500. Filters normally can't be repaired if they're broken. Just throw out the old and buy new, again around $500 to $1,000, depending on quality and type.

If the pool-cleaning robot doesn't work, consider simply throwing it away and not selling it with the home. Most buyers aren't that pool savvy. You can simply say you have a pool service to clean the pool. (A new robot can cost $400 to $700 uninstalled, assuming you already have all the equipment necessary to run it.)

I suggest that even if you've been taking care of the pool yourself, you get a pool service established for a month or two before you sell. That way you can refer any questions regarding the pool to the service.

Cracks in the pool are a serious problem. Repair can be very costly, if even possible. They can also seriously affect a sale. (I won't buy a pool home if there are cracks in the pool.)

Call a pool repair service and see what it will cost to fix the problem. Typically, the pool will have to be drained, the cracks fixed, and the pool replastered. (Today, some pool service companies can do the job underwater.) Sometimes it's simply cheaper to have the pool dug up and a lawn put in than to fix the cracks.

Leaking pipes are also a serious problem. But, because they aren't visible, you may be able to have them fixed or tied off and simply disclose the issue to the buyers.

Pools used to be a real plus when selling homes. Now, however, particularly in the southern parts of the country where so many people have had them, it's a bit different. Today, many buyers are aware of the headaches that pools offer and actually direct agents to only look for properties that don't have pools.

Thus, if you already have a pool, make sure that it's not broken. And hope for the best in attracting buyers to your property.

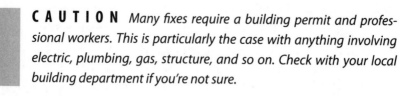

C A U T I O N *Many fixes require a building permit and professional workers. This is particularly the case with anything involving electric, plumbing, gas, structure, and so on. Check with your local building department if you're not sure.*

Fixing versus Replacing

Remember, the general rule is that if you're planning to sell, it's almost always cheaper and more cost efficient to repair than to replace. And almost always make the repairs before putting your home up for sale. To get that high offer, quick, your buyers need to see a home ready for them to move into, not one that's still under renovation.

4 When to Do It Yourself—and When to Hire Pros

SPEND LITTLE — do more.

Cost is always a big consideration when fixing up a home for sale. We all know that the less we spend, the more money will be in our pocket after the deal closes. And, of course, one of the biggest ways to save money (at least so it first appears!) is to do the fix-up work ourselves.

The big question, of course, is can, or even should, we do it? Or would it make more sense, and save money in the long run, if we hire professionals? (Keep in mind that the cost can usually be built into the sale—see Chapter 5.)

If you're in this quandary, here are some questions you should ask yourself to help make the decision:

1. *Can you spare the time?* If you're working full-time and raising a family, it may be that you only have weekends and evenings to work on the house. And that time might be better spent with the family. To get the fix-up work done quickly, it probably makes more sense to hire it out.

2. *Can you do the work?* When it comes to fixing the lawn and trimming the hedges as well as painting rooms, most of us would feel perfectly capable of doing it. But what about fixing electrical or plumbing problems? Obviously some work we can do well, and some we can't . . . and shouldn't.

3. *Can you find professionals to do the job?* These days with so many people doing fix-up work, it sometimes might take months to get a pro in to handle the work. Will this work with your timeframe for selling? You might be *forced* to do the work yourself!

4. *Will you save money?* Sometimes hiring a pro is actually cheaper than attempting to do a job yourself. For example, fixing a leaking washer in a bathroom faucet should only take half an hour and a 35-cent part. But, what if you don't have the proper wrenches or knowledge and break the faucet? Buying tools and replacing fixtures in the bathroom (remember tub, shower, and sink should match) could seem very cheap compared with the $60 to $80 plumber visit—as long as you don't mess up the job.

5. *How will it look?* This is the ultimate test. I have seen sellers spend countless hours on room renovations, wallpaper hanging, even painting—only to have the final result look amateurish and unacceptable. Buyers immediately demand it be redone. The proof is in the results, and if the results aren't of acceptable workmanship, the time, work, and money spent are wasted.

For most of us the answer to what we can or should do is a mixed bag. There are some things that, yes, we most certainly want to do ourselves. And, there are others that we definitely should hire out. What's important is not to confuse one with the other.

It Takes a Professional

There are some jobs when fixing up a property that simply require professional skill. One of them that seems like it should be the essence of simplicity is landscape design.

Many sellers tell themselves that anyone can fix up their front yard. Just mow the law, fill in the brown spots, trim the bushes, and it's done. Yes, it may very well be done. But, such a cavalier attitude may result in terrible curb appeal with the result that your home sits on the market without good offers. On the other hand, a landscape architect may suggest removing part of the lawn and replacing it with a flower bed. He or she may want to remove the shrubs to allow more of the house front to show. Tall trees may need to be cut and shorter ones planted. Removing some concrete and replacing it with stepping stones may produce a charming path to your door.

All of these are things that a landscape architect might quickly see, but that you, as the home owner, could be oblivious to. That's why getting professional help, if for no other purpose than to help with the design, can be so important.

Here's a list of other areas where professional help is usually needed:

- Designing your landscaping.
- Selecting your paint colors (and possibly painting).
- Handling electrical, plumbing, and gas fix-ups. *This is a liability issue.* You probably need a building permit and want to be protected if something later goes wrong and the house burns down, floods, or someone is injured because of work improperly done.
- Doing any plastering or wallpaper hanging.
- Installing carpeting.
- Installing kitchen countertops, cabinets, flooring, appliances, and lighting.

- Doing all carpentry.

- Performing any other complex work where the results show.

What's Your Timeframe?

In the first chapter we noted that most people who decide to sell want to do it *quick!* Most fix-up work, on the other hand, takes time and, to have a home that shows well, it should be done *before* the home is marketed. That means getting in there and doing the work right away.

But, as noted earlier, if you have a full-time job and are taking care of a family, usually you only have weekends and evenings. That may be time enough for staging, as we'll see in the next section. But, it's rarely time for more than the most cursory fix-up work.

All of which is to say that unless you've got a long timeline, forget about doing the fix-up work yourself. Plan on hiring it out.

But, you may be saying, what about the cost?

Borrow the money short term, if necessary, and pay it back from the proceeds of the sale. We'll see just how to do this in Chapter 5.

What's Your Time Worth?

Don't think that just because you do the work yourself, it's free. It's not. Your time is worth something, often something quite valuable. After all, if you weren't fixing up your house, you could be working in front of a computer, or making calls, or even just relaxing in front of the fire (relaxing is an important part of everyone's life). Whenever you do the work on the home yourself, you're trading off time that could be productively spent elsewhere.

Here's a chart to determine just how valuable your time really is.

How to Put a Value on Your Time

- *Compare it to a pro:* How much would a pro charge to do the same job you're doing? That's what your time is worth. By this standard, many sellers feel they can justify doing the work themselves (see issues of quality discussed earlier).
- *Compare it to your regular job:* How much do you make an hour? That could be what your time fixing up the house is worth (*if* you could be working at your regular job). Many sellers feel they should hire everything out when this standard is applied.
- *Compare it to a part-time job:* If you were to take on part-time work, how much could you make? In other words, how much would someone likely pay you to do the fix-up work you're contemplating doing for free? If you seriously consider this, the results may surprise you.

My suggestion is that you consider all three points in coming up with a reasonable wage for your time. Remember, it doesn't matter which of the three methods you use. They are all arbitrary. The whole point is to give yourself a wage for your work. By putting some reasonable figure down, you'll be getting a more realistic cost for fixing up your home. Then, subtract your costs for doing the work from the amount you expect to receive from the sale. This puts your equity returned to you in a more realistic perspective. It also gives you a bit of insurance. After all, what if you plan on doing some work and it turns out you can't? For example, say you're planning to paint the entire exterior of the home, and you figure your time is worth $2,000. However, on the first day you miss a step on the ladder and injure your back. Now you can't do any of the work and have to hire it out. But, you've already figured in $2,000 toward the cost, so it's not going to be quite such a financial shock.

Don't Overlook the Possibility of Injuries

No one ever expects to have an accident and be injured. That is, after all, what the word "accident" means. Yet, some accidents and injuries are positively predictable.

Consider this: a carpenter may work day in and day out building and renovating homes. She may strain to lift heavy timbers, walk on roofs, use electric equipment, and so on. Even though her trade is listed as one of the more dangerous by insurers, she may go a dozen years without an injury.

Why? Because she does it on a regular basis and knows what she's doing.

What about you, on the other hand? Do you know carpentry? Do you work physically all day long every day? (Or do you sit behind a desk?) Even if you're active, physically, doing the work of a carpenter may use different muscles and require special coordination.

In short, unless you're a carpenter yourself, chances are probably a hundred times greater that if you do a carpenter's work for just a few days, you're more likely than a real carpenter to be injured. The same holds true for every other trade that you may need to fix up your home, from laying linoleum to painting a ceiling. Your chances of injury are far greater than those for a professional doing the same job.

And if you are injured, even if it's only a sprained back or fat thumb that you hit with a hammer, it could affect your productivity at your regular job. If that happens, you'll very quickly come to realize how much your time actually is worth.

While we never plan on accidents and injuries, any time you undertake to do fix-up work on a home, you should approach the undertaking as having a high risk factor for injury—your injury.

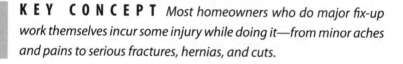

KEY CONCEPT *Most homeowners who do major fix-up work themselves incur some injury while doing it—from minor aches and pains to serious fractures, hernias, and cuts.*

What's Your Comfort Level?

For most of us, the level of comfort with fixing up a home to get it ready for sale is limited. We'll do cleaning, some painting, and fixture replacement. But, when the work gets serious, like putting in a sink and faucets or laying flooring, we want to leave it to professionals.

Of course, there are some who are the exceptions. Many home owners are born handymen. They love to tackle almost any work, know how to do it well, and can produce a quality result. If you're that sort, then by all means, proceed to do the fix-up work yourself.

Of course, the question is, how do you know which type of person you really are?

To help you determine what category you fall into, take the following quiz. There are no right or wrong answers. It may help you to get a better sense of just what amount of fixing up you want to do yourself:

Quiz: How Much Fixing Up Can You Handle?

1. Do you enjoy painting and wallpapering? ☐ Yes ☐ No

2. Do you enjoy hammering, sawing, and assembling? ☐ Yes ☐ No

3. Do you feel comfortable changing a wall switch? ☐ Yes ☐ No

4. Have you ever installed a sink, toilet, or shower? ☐ Yes ☐ No

5. Do you know how (or do you feel sure you can learn) how to remove a glass frame to get a broken window repaired? ☐ Yes ☐ No

6. Do you feel comfortable walking on a roof looking for leaks? ☐ Yes ☐ No

7. Can you plant a garden, including lawn and shrubs? ☐ Yes ☐ No

8. Could you patch and then paint the exterior of a home? ☐ Yes ☐ No

9. If a chimney were missing a few bricks, could you cement new ones in place? ☐ Yes ☐ No

10. Do you know which side of a sink is the hot water and which is cold water? ☐ Yes ☐ No

11. Is the black wire in a circuit the ground? ☐ Yes ☐ No

12. If a backyard fence had fallen over, could you sink new posts in cement and fix the fence? ☐ Yes ☐ No

13. Are you able to install a new sink and lay tile on a kitchen counter? ☐ Yes ☐ No

14. Oil-based paint is odorous and difficult to use? ☐ Yes ☐ No

15. Have you ever installed (or helped install) a furnace? A water heater? A whole-house air conditioner? ☐ Yes ☐ No

16. If you were in the attic, would you recognize a ground wire? Would you know if the ground wire were missing? ☐ Yes ☐ No

17. Could you install and populate a 200-amp circuit breaker box? (Requires professional knowledge and skills.) ☐ Yes ☐ No

18. Could you work with engineers,   ☐ Yes ☐ No
    concrete pourers, steel welders, and
    others to come up with a plan for
    stabilizing a broken foundation?

19. Would you feel comfortable   ☐ Yes ☐ No
    installing ductwork for a furnace/
    air conditioner?

20. Could you get plans, steer them   ☐ Yes ☐ No
    through building and planning
    departments, hire subcontractors
    and workers, supervise work, and
    handle problems as they appeared?

21. Do you know what a soffit, cripple,   ☐ Yes ☐ No
    and dormer are? (A soffit is the
    underside of construction such as
    a dropped ceiling. A cripple is a
    short, weaker wall. A dormer is a
    roof projection usually with a
    window. If you had to read here
    to figure these out, mark "no.")

Obviously the more times you answer "yes," the more experience and knowledge you bring to your fix-up projects. However, just because you can't answer yes to all or even most questions doesn't mean that you can't do many types of work on your own.

All of which is to say, just take this test with a big grain of salt. It doesn't prove anything about your ability to succeed. But it may show quite a bit about your current level of experience and, hence, the type of fix-up work you may be capable of doing right now.

Scoring: Count your "yes" answers, and then see what your score says about you.

Scoring

- **21 correct:** Amazing! If you're not in the building trades, you ought to be.

- **15–20:** Pretty darn good. You're definitely enthusiastic and, I suspect, have had some success as a handyman along the way. You, too, could tackle just about anything but the biggest jobs. Just be careful you don't get too confident and get in over your head.

- **10–14:** You're also an enthusiast and are probably quite handy. Try to do mostly cosmetic work. Get assistance with anything that's really big or difficult.

- **5–9:** Temper your enthusiasm with a touch of reality. Thus far, you've probably only dabbled in home fixing up. You'll probably find most of the work quite challenging.

- **0–4:** There's also room for those who sit on the sidelines and cheer. Why not take a course at a local school to learn some important handyman skills before plunging into fixing up your home?

Source: Portions of this quiz first appeared in Robert Irwin, *Find It, Buy It, Fix It,* 3rd ed. (Chicago: Dearborn Publishing, 2006).

5 Where to Get Cash for Fixing and Staging

YOU'RE GOING TO need money to do the fix-up work (and staging) that most houses need to sell quickly for top dollar. Even if you do most of it yourself, you'll still need materials and supplies, and those can be expensive.

If you're fortunate enough to have a fat bank account, then it's really a nonissue. You just write a check to cover the costs. But, what if you need to spend thousands or even tens of thousands of dollars to get your home ready to sell and you don't have the money? Do you scrimp and cut back on the work? Do you simply not do it?

I certainly hope not. We've seen that fixing up is critical to getting a good sale. And as we'll note in the next section of this book, staging is just as important.

So, where do you get the funds to do the necessary work? My suggestion is that you borrow them.

Building Equity

Most people really don't like to borrow. The reason, of course, is that when you borrow, you have to pay back the funds . . . with interest. And that's no fun!

Many sellers see borrowing to do fix-up work and staging as simply throwing good money after bad. After all, if your home is already needy, why pour more money into it? The image of a "money pit" immediately comes to mind. You'll spend more money on that old, ratty house and get even less out of it (after paying back the loan) when you sell.

Wrong!

The whole idea of spending money to fix up and stage your home is so that you'll get the top end of the price range for your home . . . and a quick sale. What that means is that, if you do the right work in the correct way, you should get back nearly all of the money you spend fixing up and staging your home . . . probably more! That, after all, is the whole point. We're not here to throw money away. We're here to make money.

Think of it this way. You have a certain amount of equity in your home (whether it be $500 or $500,000). When you do a proper job of fixing and staging, that equity increases. Do the right job and do it well, and the equity increases by the amount that you spend . . . maybe more.

Then, when you sell, you convert that equity to cash (assuming it's a cash sale which nearly all are these days). As soon as escrow closes, you get back cash not only for your original equity, but also for the increased equity from the fixing and staging.

In short, you borrow short term—then get your money back (and, hopefully, more) as soon as the property sells.

KEY CONCEPT *Even if you only break even on the amount you spend fixing and staging, you're still far ahead if you sell quickly! Remember, time is money, and the less time you have to spend selling your home, the more it should mean to you.*

In this chapter we're going to look at a variety of ways to borrow money short term to pay for fixing and staging your home.

Home Loans

Home loans go by a variety of names: "home equity loan," "home improvement loan," "institutional second mortgage," and so on. They all have one thing in common. You get a new mortgage, typically a second, from a lending institution such as a bank.

In most cases you're free to spend the money as you wish; you can even take a cruise with it. In our case, however, we're going to spend the money fixing and staging our home for sale.

Here's what you need to know about home loans *before* you obtain one:

Home Loan Facts

- *Payback:* Typically these loans are for a short timeframe—1 to 3 years (much longer than you should need to sell your home). Some, however, have a revolving feature that will last 5 to 10 years, after which they convert to a long-term ARM (adjustable rate mortgage). Because you only need the money for a short time, discuss whether having a shorter term will offer you a lower interest rate. (See the prepayment discussion.)

- *Amount:* The amount you can borrow varies according to your credit and your equity. Home loans to $500,000 and more are not uncommon. Home loans for $10,000 are just as common. Usually you can't borrow more than 80 percent (of all mortgages) of the equity in your home. For example, if you have a first mortgage in place for 70 percent of your home's value, then you can only get a home loan for 10 percent (the 70 percent first combined with the 10 percent second equal 80 percent). An appraisal is made to determine your home's value (from the lender's perspective) in relation to all financing on it.

- *Types:* There are several types of home loans. The revolving line of credit is often considered the best because you write checks on an account as you need the money. You are only charged interest on the money you actually borrow. It's like a credit card, only instead of an unsecured line of credit, your home serves as your security. Another type of loan for home improvement may be in the form of a construction loan. The money is dispersed in four or five payments, and there are specific targets (construction phases) that you must meet to get it. These are more complicated and usually require a contractor to submit a set of plans to show anticipated work.

- *Interest rate:* These home loans typically are for two or three percentage points higher than first mortgages. That, however, is often half of what credit card cash advances cost.

- *Credit:* Generally speaking you must qualify for these loans just as if you were getting a new first mortgage. A credit score of 680 or higher may be required.

- *Timeframe:* It usually takes two to three weeks to obtain a home loan from the time you apply until the time your money is actually funded and you can write a check.

- *Costs:* Typically, there are no immediate costs to you for obtaining a home loan. Rather, the lender absorbs the costs including an appraisal, credit report and credit scoring, escrow, title insurance and so on. These loans are so profitable to lenders that they are more than willing to pay for all costs, as is only appropriate.

- *Prepayment:* Today most home loan lenders will insert a clause that states that if you refinance the home loan before a set time period, say, three years, there's a monetary penalty, usually between $500 and $1,000. Many times this penalty is waived if you sell the property. Be sure to check to see if your home loan has a prepayment penalty and what its specific conditions are, or when you sell you could owe the lender extra money!

- *Payment:* Payment is usually made monthly. A percentage of the outstanding balance is calculated. Sometimes it's interest only, or it may be amortized each month over 30 years. (The payment is calculated each month as if you have 30 years to pay back the entire balance, which includes principal and interest.)

- *Tax deductibility:* The interest on your home loan *might* be deductible. This is especially the case if you use the money to improve your property. However, there are limitations and the Tax Code on this subject is more complex than most people realize—sometimes the money is *not* tax deductible. See a tax professional for advice.

- *Existing mortgages:* Usually the lender will insist on a second mortgage (or a first). If you already have a second mortgage on your property, the lender may pay it off and add the amount to the balance of your new home loan making additional cash available to you.

- *Sources*
  - Savings and loans (sometimes called mutual banks)
  - Mortgage brokers or bankers
  - Banks
  - Commercial credit companies
  - Credit unions (you must be a member)
  - Private lenders (check with title insurance companies for sources)

Home Loan Advantages

There are many advantages to a home loan.

- You get the money quickly, usually within a few weeks.
- You may be able to borrow as much as you want to do all the work.
- You can borrow only as much as you need and, hence, are not paying interest on money not used.
- The interest rate is usually reasonable, close to what a new first mortgage will cost.

Home Loan Disadvantages

There are also some disadvantages:

- The money is not instantaneous, as it would be by borrowing from an existing credit card.
- There may be a prepayment penalty.
- If you have a small equity in your home (under 20 percent), you may not be able to get a home loan.

Credit Cards

Most of us have credit cards. For fixing and staging, it's often possible to use them to finance the work. You can buy materials outright with the cards, and you can get a cash advance to cover money you'll need to pay workers.

Normally, most people wisely do not use a credit card to purchase anything large for the home. The reason is that credit cards are intended for short-term borrowing, and home improvement is typically longer term.

That's not the case here, however. Here, we're planning to use the money short term, hopefully just a month or so until the home is sold. As soon as that happens, the money borrowed and credit used can be paid back to the credit cards.

Credit Card Advantages

- You can borrow up to the cards' limits without regard to the equity in your home. Thus, if you have little equity, it shouldn't affect your ability to borrow.
- The money is instantaneous (assuming you have credit cards in place that have available balances). With a credit card, you can start work tomorrow.
- The cards are universally accepted, so you won't have trouble buying paint or windows or lumber or whatever.
- The minimum payment required each month is usually quite low when compared with the outstanding balance.

Credit Card Disadvantages

- The interest rate can be high, 20 to 30 percent annually in some cases, depending on your credit. However, you may be willing to pay it for a short time until your home is fixed and staged and sells.
- If you max out your credit cards, it could adversely affect your credit when you attempt to get a new first mortgage on the purchase of your next home.
- You may worry about the amount you are charging. This affects a few people who can't sleep nights worrying about their credit card debt. If this is you, then you're better off not using your credit cards.

Government Loans

There are a host of government programs designed especially to help sellers/home owners who need help in rehabilitating their homes. The two largest are FHA Title 1 and FHA Section 203K. In most cases of loans with the Federal Housing Administration (FHA), the loans are only insured by the FHA; the money is actually funded by a bank.

Under Title 1, the loan must be used exclusively for fix-up work. There is a maximum loan amount, $25,000, and there are other conditions; for example, the property must be your principal residence. (There are provisions for investor lending, but these are less often used.)

Unlike bank home loans, the maximum combined mortgages can be up to 100 percent of the property's value (combined mortgage[s] plus home improvement loan). The maximum term is 20 years, and the interest rate is competitive. For more detailed information you can check *www.hud.gov.*

The Section 203K loan program is likewise available only to home owners who reside on the property and is used primarily for the rehabilitation of single family homes. Here, however, you get the loan at the time you acquire the property. (One loan is granted both to buy and then to fix up the house.)

The amount of the mortgage is based on the projected value of the property after all the work is completed. In other words, it takes into account the cost of the fix-up work, not just the property's current condition.

The property must be a one- to four-unit structure (condos qualify) and at least one year old. The maximum loan cannot exceed the cost of the property plus fix-up work, or 110 percent of the property's anticipated value after fix-up.

Money is advanced to pay off the property, and the amount designated for fix-up is placed into an escrow account and then released as work is completed, according to a plan created by the borrower and approved by the FHA. The maximum loan amount is the same as that for the 203b program, which varies by state and county. For more information, check into *www.hud.gov/fha/203K.*

Advantages of FHA Loans

- You can get funding for 100 percent (or more) of the value of the property.
- Interest rates are competitive.

Disadvantages of FHA Loans

- There are many restrictions.
- Getting appraisals and filling out forms can be a nightmare. You should find an institutional lender who handles these on a regular basis and knows the ropes.
- It can take many months before you actually get funded.

Additional Government Loans

Fannie Mae (*www.fanniemae.com*) and Freddie Mac (*www.freddiemac.com*) offer similar programs, sometimes with financing in excess of 100 percent of the property's value! There are also many state, city, and municipal programs. You will need to check with your city's housing office to find out about these.

Other Sources of Financing

It's important to remember that when you only need the money for a short time, there are always myriad ways to raise it. Here are some options you may not have considered (or may not want to consider—but remember, hopefully it's only short term):

- *Relatives and friends:* Yes, I know, it's a pain to ask, but sometimes making the effort will result in getting the money you need right away. Besides, think of how much your family status will be enhanced when your house sells and you pay the money back . . . with interest!

- *Sell something:* Do you have an old motorcycle, motor home, boat, or other item that can be quickly sold for a few thousand dollars? Consider doing so. Yes, you may hate to part with it, but you probably can buy a better one once your home sells.

- *Assets:* Do you have a coin or stamp collection, stocks and bonds, bullion, or other assets? Consider either taking an asset-based loan out on these or selling them outright. Banks often make short-term asset-based loans for a low interest rate.

- *Retirement accounts:* Be careful here: you never want to risk money that you can't replace. Check with your accountant first. Remember, there may be penalties (although these can sometimes be avoided by borrowing against funds, or taking them out and quickly returning them within a month or two).

Always Have a "Back-Door Plan"

A word of caution. There's always a chance, no matter how slim, that no matter how much work you do, your house simply won't sell.

You might be in a terrible market where nothing is selling (except, of course, for properties where the sellers are simply giving away their homes.) You might have a terrible negative influence nearby (toxic dump site; high-voltage electrical wires; even horrible neighbors who leave cars, furniture, and garbage strewn in front of their house) that discourages all buyers. Or, you simply might be unlucky. These are the sorts of things that are difficult to overcome.

What do you do if you've borrowed money to fix and stage, and then, no matter how hard you and your agent try, your house simply doesn't sell? What do you do about the debt you've incurred?

The answer is what I call a "back-door plan." It's having a way to convert the short-term expensive borrowing you've made into a long-term, low interest rate loan (meaning low-payment borrowing). It's a plan so that if the worst arises, you can still hang onto the house, live there, and thrive.

Usually it involves refinancing. If you can refi into a 30-year mortgage, you can spread that debt over a long period, and the payments won't be so onerous. Check with a good mortgage broker *before* you make that short-term loan to be sure that in an emergency you can convert it to long-term financing.

PART TWO

Stage It!

6 What Staging Can Do for You

IT'S ALL ABOUT beating out the competition.

You don't sell your home in a vacuum. The average buyer who comes to see your place has seen (or will see) anywhere from 7 to 41 homes before making a purchase decision. The old idea that a buyer falls in love with the first place he or she sees is bunk. (That's not to say it can't happen—you just don't want to wait for it to happen.) Today's buyers are savvy and see all the homes in the neighborhood before they make an offer. Therefore, your goal is to beat out all that competition.

Think of it from a buyer's perspective. A buyer wants as much bang for the buck as he or she can get. If there are two similar homes at close to the same price, one that shows beautifully and the other that shows just OK, that buyer is going to go with the home that shows best every time.

It all comes down to the fact that *visual value sells*. And staging is what allows the visual value of your house to shine through.

Also keep in mind that unlike when there was a shortage of homes, in today's more balanced market with more equal numbers of buyers and sellers, buyers feel they can afford to get fussy. If a home doesn't look just perfect, they feel they can look elsewhere. If they don't buy your home, there are many others to choose from.

 KEY CONCEPT *Buyers think of homes as "good ones" and "bad ones." You want your home to be considered the former, not the latter.*

When to Stage

Once you make the decision to sell, it's important that you not rush into listing and putting your home on the market. Nothing does more to harm a sale than to have a shabby-looking house out there. Yes, the sellers may say they'll fix it up within the next few weeks. But, buyers don't see that. They only see a work in progress—a fixer. And that means a low offer.

Tad and Shirley are good examples of this. They owned a small home on the outskirts of Philadelphia. Shirley got a new job in New Jersey, and they decided to move rather than have her make a long commute. They put a deposit on a new home and hoped to sell their old one immediately.

They'd lived there for 11 years, and like many of us, had deferred maintenance. Their basement needed repairs because of water damage. The interior and exterior of their home needed painting. They had it stuffed with furniture they had acquired through purchases and hand-me-downs from relatives. And there was other staging that needed doing (see Chapters 7 and 8).

Yet, instead of fixing and staging, they went right to selling. An agent warned them that the house did not show well, but took the listing anyway. And the house sat there with few lookers and no offers.

During the first month, Tad and Shirley spent their time fixing and staging the property. It took them nearly five weeks, but when it was done, the place was a showcase. The problem was that by then it was a *stale* listing.

Agents who had buyers who might have been interested had already previewed the place and determined it didn't look good enough to show. Shirley and Tad's house became known as a "stinker." Even though now it was fixed up and their agent touted the fact that it looked much better, the word had gotten out. Nobody wanted to show it.

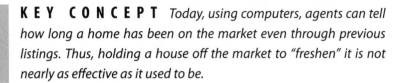

K E Y   C O N C E P T *A stale listing is one that has been on the market for more than a month or two. Because it hasn't sold, buyers and agents often consider that there's something wrong with the property, or the price, or both. Hence, they don't even bother to come by and look at it.*

The listing ran for three months and then expired. The agent wanted them to renew, but a different agent told them they'd be wise to keep the home off the market for at least a month before listing again.

They did, with the new agent, and at a lower price. Coming out as a new listing, many agents checked it out and were pleased with how it showed. They brought their buyers to see it. This time the house sold within a week.

K E Y   C O N C E P T *Today, using computers, agents can tell how long a home has been on the market even through previous listings. Thus, holding a house off the market to "freshen" it is not nearly as effective as it used to be.*

The moral of the story? Tad and Shirley lost more than four months of time and quite possibly a higher price by putting their home on the market before it was fixed, staged, and ready to show. Yes, you want to sell quickly. But, no, you shouldn't list and put on the market a house that's not ready to show. It will only delay a sale and make it more difficult to get your price.

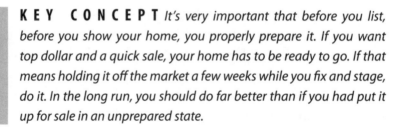

K E Y   C O N C E P T *It's very important that before you list, before you show your home, you properly prepare it. If you want top dollar and a quick sale, your home has to be ready to go. If that means holding it off the market a few weeks while you fix and stage, do it. In the long run, you should do far better than if you had put it up for sale in an unprepared state.*

Caught in Our Own Lifestyle

You can think of staging as nothing more than thinking outside the box. The box, in this case, is the way we live in our home.

If you've lived in your home for more than six months, you've made it comfortable . . . for you. You probably have your favorite furniture, perhaps an old easy chair that's been around for a while that's just perfect for watching television. Along the way, maybe you or your kids or spouse have put your feet up on the coffee table while relaxing, and it has a few scratches. Maybe there's a beer or wineglass stain on an end table, coffee stains on the carpet, or a broken lamp by the door.

K E Y   C O N C E P T *Real estate agents are always quick to suggest that the way to sell is to drop your price. A better way is to improve your product.*

The list is really endless. As we live in a house, we "break it in." That means we make is as comfortable a place for us to live as possible. Then, when it's time to sell, we wonder why buyers don't see the place as we do. After all, if it's just right for us, how could it not be just right for others?

As I say, most of us get caught up in our lifestyle when what we really need to be thinking about it how to present our home to buyers. And that takes some thinking outside the box.

Getting a New Perspective on Your Home

- Try to think outside your own shoes—of how strangers might see your home.

- Ask others, particularly professionals. As we'll see later in this chapter, you can hire stagers to come in and give you ideas. Agents see countless houses and often can give you good ideas. Be sure to ask.

- Check out model homes—don't pass by a housing tract with model homes. Check them out. Usually each model home has been professionally staged. Borrow ideas from them.

- Sit in different areas, corners, and chairs in your house. Simply seeing things from another angle can help.

- Go outside and look in through your windows. You may be surprised at how your house looks from the new perspective.

What Does Staging Involve?

Staging of homes to sell actually began in earnest about 20 years ago. It happened first in south Florida and in southern California, mainly to very expensive homes.

The seller would hire a decorator to come and, in essence, redecorate the interior of the home. (Sometimes landscape architects would be hired to reshape the exterior of the property as well.) New furnishings would come in: new carpeting and wall hangings and so on. It wasn't uncommon to spend anywhere from $10,000 to $40,000 to stage a home. Of course, if the property were selling in the millions, it was considered money well spent.

Real estate agents quickly caught on that a properly staged home would sell quicker and for more money. And they began spreading the word among their clients. Soon, across the country and in all price ranges, savvy sellers began "staging."

Of course, they didn't usually spend tens of thousands of dollars. They took the ideas of the stagers and applied them in a low-cost way to their own homes. They quickly found out that there were certain rules of staging that applied to all homes, whether high priced or low. And most of these did not require a great deal of expense to be carried out. Here are some of the basic tenets of staging:

- *Get back to basics:* Return the rooms in your home to their intended use. If you're using a family room as a place to keep your pool table, bring it back to being a family room. If a bedroom is used for storage, remake it as bedroom. Yes, sometimes conversions do make sense as in the case of a home office, but most of the time they're just a convenience to promote our own lifestyle. If you bring the home back to its intended use, you usually bring back some of the original attraction of it.

- *Uncover the architectural details:* Don't try to turn a peach into a lemon or a Craftsman-style home into a Southern Plantation style. Each home has its own architectural style. Over time, often style details get covered up with paint, veneers, and clutter. Bring them back, and you'll return to the charm of the original home.

- *Highlight the best features:* What is most appealing about your home? Is it a large living space? A wonderful master bedroom? The floor plan? Stone countertops? The backyard? The carpeting? Discover the best features of your home and then highlight them. It's the same as going with your strengths and avoiding your weaknesses. Make potential buyers see the best your home has to offer.

- *Defuse your décor:* For nearly all of us, our furniture, drapery, colors, and so on, reflect our personal tastes. But, to find a buyer you need them to appeal to a broad range of people. That means to make them more neutral, less potentially offensive to others.

- *De-personalize:* Everything in your home says *you*—from the clothing in your closets to the pictures on your nightstand. You want it instead to be open, ready for the next person, the buyer.

These are the big five when it comes to staging. Accomplish them and you'll probably move your home the first weekend! In the following chapters, we'll have much more to say about how to accomplish the five rules, but first, let's talk about professional stagers.

In most areas of the country, there are people who, for a fee (typically around $300 to $500, but often tied to the size of the home), will come in and tell you what to do to stage your property. They'll usually go room to room and make a list of what needs to be done. If they're any good, they'll present you with several sheets of paper outlining exactly what your home needs.

Then, you can either do it yourself, or, for a much more substantial fee, they'll actually do it all. They'll stage for you what you can stage for yourself. For those who don't have the time and do have the funds, this is probably the easiest and most efficient way to go. For the rest of us, read on.

Stagers

You can check the local phone book for "Stagers" and "Home staging." You can also use those keywords in searching the Internet. And often real estate agents can give you the names of successful stagers they have worked with who specialize in your area. The following websites were active as of this writing for stagers:

- *www.stagedhomes.com*
- *www.homestagingsource.com*
- *www.howtohomestage.com*

7 Ten Tricks for Saving Time and Money on Staging

YOU CAN DO it—and you can do it yourself.

Of course, you must know what to do, and that's what we'll discover in this chapter. Here are the 10 most important tricks for staging your house. Do them all and you can begin counting off the days until your sale.

Remember, you can't count on buyers to have an imagination. They won't see how your home will be after the work is done—they'll only see how it is now. So make the "now" as perfect as you can. Think of it as if you were detailing your car, inside and out. Make it shine. Show it off to its best advantage:

1. Remove clutter

2. Depersonalize

3. Clean and wash

4. Universalize colors

5. Update lighting

6. Change wall and window coverings and ceiling appearance

7. Deodorize

8. Add flower color

9. Change furniture and accessorize

10. Control temperature and noise

1. Remove Clutter

Clutter is probably your biggest enemy. It stifles your house, fills it up, and makes it appear unlivable to others. And the most insidious thing about it is that we are usually oblivious to our own clutter. While any potential buyer coming to see our house immediately recognizes it, we who live there day in and day out tend to overlook it.

 KEY CONCEPT *I always advise sellers as a rule-of-thumb to simply take one-third of all their furnishings and move them out. The house will then seem empty to you, but just right to buyers.*

What Is Clutter?

Keeping in mind that most of us don't easily recognize clutter, here's what to look for in your home:

Too Much Furniture. Too many pieces of furniture in a room is typical. When we first move in, we'll often have minimal furniture. Then, as time goes by, we buy a piece here and there. Sometimes we inherit some pieces from relatives. We may not even throw out old furniture: when it comes time to replace an old stuffed chair, we may realize it really is the most comfortable in the room, so we hang onto it . . . along with its replacement. After a while, each room is overflowing with furniture. I've been in some homes where you can barely weave a path from one end to the other, it's so cluttered with furnishings.

The Wrong Furniture. Few of us can afford to have an interior decorator come in and "design" our living space. For most of us, it's a matter of dragging our old furniture, accumulated over time, from the last home we sold to the next home we buy. As a result, often the old furniture is simply too big to fit, or awkward, or the wrong style, or it's incredibly dated. Or perhaps we buy something on sale—a chair here, a chest of drawers there, a couch someplace else. The best thing that can be said is that our furniture is "eclectic." The worst is that it's a hodge-podge of styles, colors, materials, and pieces. Get rid of everything that's mismatched and detracts from the room.

Don't overlook patio furniture. Many of us keep old patio furniture long after it's useful life has expired. It may be faded from being in the sunlight, ripped and torn, broken—yet it's still out in the patio cluttering up our yard.

Boxes. I have friends who still haven't opened all their boxes from the time they moved into their current house, even though it's been nearly 10 years! Further, if you're selling, then you're planning to move and chances are you may have already started packing in anticipation—more boxes!

Boxes do not, in any way, enhance the appearance of your home. Rather, they fill up rooms and make them look smaller, are generally unattractive, and give potential buyers the wrong idea: that you're anxious to move, hence perhaps a low-ball offer is in order. Remove *all* boxes.

Doodads. This is a catch-all phrase I like to use for trinkets, cups, clocks, mantle pieces, ceramics, glass pieces, and on and on that we all tend to put on mantles, shelves, and virtually any other surface. I have some friends who must have thousands of these covering every square inch of available space in their home.

They love them. But would-be buyers wonder where in the world they would put their own doodads? The effect is to make the home look very much like a cluttered antique store. Would you want to move into an antique store? Make them go away.

Clothing. How can clothing be clutter? Consider this: you walk into someone else's home and happen to look in their closet. What do you think if it's jam-packed with clothing—clothing bulging from hangers, on shelves, on the floor in shoe boxes, and on and on? You think two things: these people have too much clothing (irrelevant to selling the home), and there's too little closet space for me (very relevant to selling). Remove much of your clothing.

Tools and Things. It's not just the inside of your home that can be overwhelmed with clutter. It's also the garage and yard. A big problem is having too many tools, paint cans, rakes, boxes, and so on. There may be leaves and other debris in the side yards, places that typically seem to attract old pieces of wood, roofing, tar, and other clutter. Get rid of it all during the sales process.

When Do You Get Rid of Clutter?

If you're like me, you tend to put off many things that seem burdensome to do. Removing clutter is probably high on the list of those things. Why bother with it today when tomorrow will do?

The problem, of course, is that when you're selling your house, tomorrow is when buyers are coming by. And the last thing you want to be doing is getting rid of that clutter with a buyer looking over your shoulder. It's kind of like sitting in a restaurant watching the chef and staff bring the meat and fish to be prepared for the dinner through the dining room. Or looking at a new building that's only half finished.

Any would-be buyers are going to say to themselves, "I'd better wait on this place until they've finished getting it ready." In the meantime, of course, they're on to a dozen other homes that have already been decluttered, and yours never gets seen by them again.

Do it before you show your home. Do it before you list your property. Do it before you put your home up for sale. Getting an early start, here, pays off.

What to Do with It?

OK, we know what clutter is. Now, how do we get rid of it?

The hardest part is making the decision to act. Many of the things that I've described as clutter, you might think of as heirlooms. Indeed, some of the items might have been handed down to you from generations ago. They are precious. You can't just discard them . . . or can you?

It's important to remember your goal here. You want to sell your home. And if clutter is keeping it from getting sold, well then clutter must go, even if it includes fond things.

KEY CONCEPT *I've found that the "rule-of-the-whole" works best here. If you have to pick and choose between what to keep in your house and what to get rid of, almost always you will keep too much. On the other hand, if you bite the bullet and simply say, "It's all got to go," your job becomes easier. You won't agonize over individual items. Just pack it all up and move it out.*

Here's what you can do with the clutter you have:

- *Store it:* You can rent a space in a mini-warehouse storage facility in almost any city or town these days for a minimal price. Just carefully box up your clutter and then store it. Once you sell your old home, you can move it to your new one and clutter the new place up all over again.

CAUTION *Some advisers suggest you neatly store your clutter in boxes in closets, in the attic, in the basement, in the garage, even in sheds in the yard.* Don't shift it around! *You're just moving clutter from one area to another. And you'll make your closets, attic, basement, yard, or wherever look cluttered, WHICH will detract from the appearance of your home. If at all possible, move the clutter off*

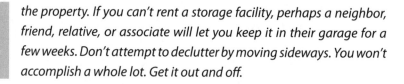

the property. If you can't rent a storage facility, perhaps a neighbor, friend, relative, or associate will let you keep it in their garage for a few weeks. Don't attempt to declutter by moving sideways. You won't accomplish a whole lot. Get it out and off.

- *Throw it away:* This can often be the hardest thing to do. But, you have to ask yourself, "Do I really need this? Will it actually look good in my new home? Will I ever use it again?" Sometimes the best alternative to storage is dumping. I've got some old ski boots, poles, and skis from 20 years ago. The equipment is outdated and possibly dangerous. Yet I've hung onto it with the dream of going back to skiing. I would probably be a whole lot better off realizing that if I haven't skied in the last 20 years, I'm probably unlikely to do it in the next 20. And if I do, on such an infrequent basis, maybe renting would be a whole lot better than hanging onto archaic equipment. Throwing out our precious things can sometimes be heart rending. But, often it's just what's needed to make us move on—and to give us a quicker sale.

- *Give it to others:* There are usually a lot of people out there with a lot less than what we have. Often our discards can be important to them. Make a donation of your clutter and you're not only sharpening your property, but doing a good deed as well. Besides, you might be able to get a tax deduction for it! (Check with your accountant first as the rules for charitable donations seem to change all the time.)

C A U T I O N *Don't have a garage sale while your home is for sale. It will distract potential buyers and could mess up a potential sale.*

- *Sell it:* Participate in the good old-fashioned American tradition of a garage sale. Drag your excess furniture, clothing, doodads, and anything else onto your driveway for a

Saturday and Sunday display. Who knows, you might actually make some money from it. Other opportunities for selling come from *eBay.com, CraigsList.com,* and local newspapers that specialize in moving small items.

2. Depersonalize

When you move into a new home, your first activity is usually to make it your own—make it "homey." That means to personalize it: put your things everywhere so it reminds you of, well, you.

Unfortunately, that's exactly the opposite of what you need to do to sell your home. When buyers comes through, you want them to see where they can put *their* personal things. You want buyers to be thinking, "Our sofa will fit well against that wall," or, "We can put all of your golfing trophies on that shelf," or, "Our clothing will fit nicely in this walk-in closet."

What should be obvious is that there's a problem here. If your personal items are all over the house, there's simply not going to be enough room (even virtual room) for the buyer's personal stuff. Something's simply not going to fit. And it's going to be the buyer's stuff. Which, of course, means that you're not going to get the sale you, as a seller, want.

To avoid this problem, you need to depersonalize your home. You need to go through and remove all those things that remind you of . . . well, you. Simply box them up and store them away from the house. That way buyers won't see them, won't be put off by them, and won't hesitate to make you a good purchase offer.

Here's a list of what to remove to depersonalize your home:

- *Photos:* Get rid of photo albums; pictures of your car or boat; graphic representations of any kind showing you, your family, or what you own. When you start looking, you'll be surprised at how many of these are hung on walls and scattered through your house. (By the way, you can leave your wedding photo on the nightstand near your bed—most buyers will understand.)

- *Trophies:* You may have a bookcase full of these from your own successes, your children's winnings, or others in the family. They really are wonderful, and I fully applaud your desire to share them. Just don't share them with a buyer who wants to put his or her own trophies in the same case.

- *Degrees:* OK, you've got your PhD, or your Masters, or your AA or your certificate of something-or-other. You're most certainly to be complimented on your achievement. It's a big step and we all know it. Only buyers really don't care. It doesn't enter into the sale of your home. And, it just might intimidate someone who wants to make an offer. Don't think of it as hiding them. Just put them away until later in your new home.

- *Medicines:* So you take medicine on a daily basis. So do most people, including your author. But don't leave the medicine containers out on the nightstand, the bathroom countertop, or a chest of drawers. No, it's not that a buyer wandering through might take them; while that's possible it's highly unlikely. Rather, potential buyers will see the medicines and decide that it's a sick person's room, no matter how innocuous they may be. And once they decide it's a sick person's room, they won't want to be in it. And there's another nail in the coffin of your sale. Put those medicines in the medicine cabinet in the bathroom or in a drawer somewhere. But get them out of sight.

- *Books:* It's OK to leave books out, if they're classics. But, if they are current books, it might just turn out that the potential buyer has different tastes and just might not approve of the books you read. Is that possible? It certainly is in the three areas of concern: religion, sex, and politics. Simply remove any books on these topics from your home. If you want books, settle for romances, mysteries, or science fiction. Coffee table picture books about architecture are a sure winner.

- *Religious icons:* Unless you feel you must leave these up for religious reasons, my suggestion is that you temporarily take them down until you've got a sale. This is not because I'm irreligious: I'm not. It's simply because the person who may want to buy your home may be of a different faith and seeing your icons can unconsciously affect his or her desire to purchase. I can recall showing a home once where the sellers had a small Buddhist shrine in the bedroom where incense was burning. My buyers never said a word, but couldn't wait to get onto the next house.

- *Shoes and clothing:* This applies mostly to children, especially teenagers, and a few husbands. While we talked about having too much clothing in your closets, I now refer to having clothing and shoes scattered on the floor of a bedroom, at the entrance to the garage, entrance to the house, or as you come into the house from the patio. Teenagers in particular seem to universally love to throw their clothes off and let them lay where they fall. And some husbands keep extra pairs of work shoes and home slippers at critical entrances to the house. I know it's difficult, nearly impossible, but clean these up. Even if you just scoop up all the clothes and stick them in the washing machine and throw all the shoes in a bin, do it before any buyer sees the house. It's a small thing, but it can make a big difference.

- *Jewelry:* You may have some costume jewelry or even the real thing that you wear on a regular basis. For convenience, you probably keep it out in the open on your bureau. Don't. There are actually two reasons, here. The first is security. Remember, even though they are presumably buyers, you're going to be showing your home to strangers. They are going to be walking around its various rooms. While a good real estate agent will attempt to keep an eye on them at all times, occasionally they may be alone. And once in a rare while, something of value disappears from a home. The other reason is that jewelry personifies you. And remember, we're trying to depersonalize. Put all your valuables together at a different location. And conceal any jewelry you must keep in your home. Put it at the back of a drawer or, if you have one, in a safe. You'll lessen the chances of anything getting stolen. And you'll increase the prospects of getting an offer.

3. Clean and Wash

I have a real estate agent friend who provides this service automatically for all her listings. As soon as she lists a property, she sends out a crew who thoroughly wash the kitchen (including the sink), the bathrooms (including the toilets), and the floors except for carpeting, which they vacuum. It costs her about $200 a house, but she says it ensures that the home will show well. It's her little contribution to staging.

You can do the same thing for yourself, or you can call a service for a similar amount to do it for you. (They are readily available in the yellow pages of your local phone book or on the Internet.) The advantage of a service is that they are quick, they already have all the right chemicals, and presumably, they know what they're doing.

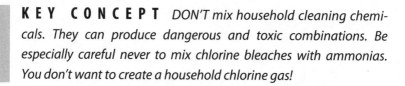

KEY CONCEPT *DON'T mix household cleaning chemicals. They can produce dangerous and toxic combinations. Be especially careful never to mix chlorine bleaches with ammonias. You don't want to create a household chlorine gas!*

These are the basics that every house should have done. Would-be buyers expect at the very least that the home they are going to look at is clean. If it's not, they'll downgrade it in their opinion and often simply not consider it.

Beyond basic cleaning and washing in bathrooms and kitchen, here are other areas that you will want to pay special attention to:

- *Carpets:* If you're not going to replace them, as suggested in Chapter 3, have them thoroughly cleaned. This is particularly the case with wall-to-wall carpeting. Beware of "steam machines." In my experience they tend to imbed the dirt deeper in the carpet. Some of the new dry chemical cleaners work very well and aren't messy. Your choice is usually to rent a cleaner at a local supermarket or hire someone to come in and do the job for a few hundred dollars. If you can find a good carpet cleaner on the basis of solid recommendations, I suggest you hire it out. Having a pro do it usually gives the best results. And it's not really that expensive.

- *Door hardware:* Sometimes dirt and grit get embedded on and around door handles. Besides looking bad, they can actually become grimy and sticky. Be sure to clean them with a good degreaser. This especially the case for your front door.

- *Railings:* Used for going up and down staircases, the paint or stain often wears off, and they get streaked. Degrease and then, if necessary, repaint or restain.

- *Windows:* Many owners only clean the windows on their home once or twice a year. Be sure to do it before you put the place up for sale. Sellers will look in, and look out. If all they see is a muddy haze, it's not going to improve their perception of your property. Carefully clean all windows as well as window screens. (Replace worn or broken screens as necessary.)

- *Fixtures and faucets:* Water faucets often get streaked with calcium deposits. Sometimes chemicals in the water can dis-color them. Usually a thorough cleaning will do the trick here. If not, you may need to have them replaced.

- *Walls:* This is the great no man's land of cleaning. What do you do about marks, scratches, and stains on walls? (We already discussed fixing any holes in walls in Chapter 3.) If it's a bathroom and there's a high-gloss paint on the walls, almost always the marks and stains can be removed with a good deter-gent cleaner and some elbow grease. (Scratches will probably require repainting the wall, or at least some retouching.)

The walls in the rest of the house, however, are a different kind of problem. Most of the time these are painted with a flat wall paint. This paint can seldom be washed or cleaned. Any detergent or degreaser you use is likely to leave a mark. And scrubbing only removes the paint. My suggestion is to avoid working hard at it and then being upset with the result. Don't clean and wash, but instead repaint. (By the way, crayons present a special problem. They often bleed right through a new coat of paint. Try sealing them first with clear spray shellac, then painting over them. You'll be surprised at the results.)

- *Appliances:* Yes, you're going to have to clean that oven, and be sure it's spotless. Chances are at least one of the buyers will open the over door to look inside and may even run a finger across the surface. How clean your oven is may determine how buyers see the cleanliness of your home overall. There are heavy-duty cleaners that will do the job. But, they tend to be caustic, so use gloves and caution. Also clean the refrigerator, dishwasher, and any other appliances you have in your kitchen. The good news is that, typically, these appliances have hard, glossy surfaces and clean up very well.

- *Countertops:* If you have stone or laminate, it's usually just a matter of washing and putting away pots, pans, dishes, and small appliances and then giving the top a quick wipe. If you have tile, it's a different story. The problem, as you undoubtedly realize, is grout. The grout, especially if it's light colored, tends to accumulate dirt and grease and darken, making the most outstanding part of your countertop the dirty grout. It makes your entire kitchen look dirty, tired, and undesirable.

Cleaning methods include scraping off the top surface of the grout with a putty knife or wire brush or using some sort of electric wire brush. In extreme cases, the old grout can be removed and the tile regrouted. That, however, tends to be expensive and often results in broken tiles that can't easily be replaced. I've found all of these to be of limited value. What really works for me is a mild solution of bleach spread over the tiles and grout and allowed to sit for a while. This has the effect of bleaching the grout to a lighter color. (Of course, if you have colored grout, it may bleach it to a color you don't want, so try it out on a small section, first!) Use gloves, avoid the fumes, and be careful!

- *Cabinets:* This is a back-breaking job. In the kitchen and sometimes in the bathroom, food and other detritus tend to get splashed around and stuck on the cabinet doors as well as in the cabinets themselves. Over time, it accumulates until the cabinets simply look filthy. Filthy cabinets do not a house sell. You need to clean them.

    There are many cleaners that do a good job. However, you do need to go over all of the surfaces with a scrub sponge and, in many cases, apply a little elbow grease. They'll look great when you're finished, but you may need a couple of aspirin for your back.

- *Floors:* For linoleum and some synthetic woods, wash and polish. (But be careful not to make them slippery—having a buyer slip and hit her head is not a good way to get an offer.) For tile, cleaning usually works well, but remember to make the grout look good. For stone, follow the recommendations of the installer.

4. Universalize Colors

Are some colors traditional, some modern, and others simply old-fashioned?

Sort of. Some colors are associated with certain eras. For example, there was a time back in the 1970s when every appliance sold seemed to be avocado green. A few years later, they were all yellow. Today, bright white, stainless steel, and black seem the rule.

The same holds true with exterior home colors. In California, for example, from about 1970 to 1990 a vast preponderance of homes seemed to be colored light brown on the stucco and oxford (deep) brown on the trim. After that, Spanish pinks and yellows came into vogue. And more recently, greens and grays have made a big appearance.

Of course, the colors found on homes in different areas will vary. But someone who's adept at knowing colors can frequently walk into a neighborhood and tell when the homes were built simply by the color choices that the builder made.

Thus, if you're going to be painting the exterior of your home, my suggestion is that you check with a pro. Often times, large paint stores have color designers who can help you make modern choices, such as:

- Sherwin-Williams
- Benjamin Moore
- Dunn-Edwards
- Behr

A word of caution, however. If you belong to a homeowner's association (have a condo or a community-type home), be sure to check with the architectural committee first. Frequently, associations have strict, even if sometimes outdated, rules regarding the colors you can use.

For interior colors, however, it tends to be a different story. Today's modern rooms typically have lighter ceilings and darker walls. And in every room one wall tends to be an accent color. That's a lot of careful painting to do. Or, when you paint the interior of your home, you can go with "the real estate agent's choice": paint the entire home beige or off-white. Beige and off-white are neutral colors and, as such, tend to be less offensive than any strong color such as red, yellow, green, and so on. On the other hand, beige has been used so much that it tends to make me sick. I hate homes that are all beige.

Therefore, my suggestion is that because you need a neutral color, you go with an off-white. Stark white (called such things as snow, artic, bright, etc., by paint companies) is the color of kitchen appliances and is simply too bold for most rooms. Buyers might be repelled by it. Adding, however, a touch of yellow and brown tones the white down just a bit. You don't get into the ubiquitous beige, but you have a pleasant, *neutral* color that isn't like to offend anyone. Paint the trim in a glossy version of the same color and you're done.

On the other hand, perhaps you're an artist, a genius with color, someone who understands shades and tones and subtleties. Then, by all means experiment with different colors in your house. Just be aware, however, that no matter what colors you choose (unless they're off-white or, ughh, beige) you're sure to offend some buyer.

5. Update Lighting

It's a maxim that light sells, darkness doesn't. If your home is dark in the inside, you need to do some work on it if you want it to sell.

The old real estate agent's trick is to call the sellers before showing the home and say, "I'll be out in 15 minutes. Turn on all the lights!" The idea, of course, is that by the time the agent brings the buyers by, the home will all be lit up and bright and will show well. You, of course, should do the same thing. Any time you know that buyers are coming to look, be sure all your lights are on. This is not the time to worry about spending a extra few bucks on electricity—consider it a cost of getting the sale.

Before you even list the property, however, you should spend a few moments doing an inventory to see if you have adequate lighting throughout. Go into each room and turn on all the lights. Are the rooms bright? No, of course you don't want it so dazzling that it hurts your eyes. But, is there plenty of warm light?

Most rooms have dark corners, and most houses have dark rooms. Now's the time to stage those areas. While putting in a skylight is nice, usually you don't have to go to such an extreme. Simply add additional lighting.

All modern homes have wall plugs every 12 feet along the walls. Buy some table lamps and some free-standing lamps, and place them in each room's dark areas. You can purchase them for around $50 apiece at such places as Lowe's and Home Depot. The light fixtures don't need to be particularly stylish; in fact, it's better if they're plain in appearance.

 KEY CONCEPT *Lighting fixtures should be placed and the design should not be noticed. You want them to highlight the room, not themselves.*

Also, check the wattage of the bulbs in existing fixtures. Whenever possible, go with the maximum wattage the fixture can handle. Over time, many people replace old light bulbs with new ones of lower wattage simply because of convenience or to save on their electricity costs. Now is not the time to do that. Bump up the wattage and/or lumens of bulbs where possible. That way you'll get more light from your existing fixtures.

Also, try to avoid fluorescents wherever possible. While some of the newer ones have a more pleasant yellow light, the older ones tend to have a harsh white light that many people find annoying. You don't want to annoy your potential buyer.

A word about energy conservation. Most of what I've said here about lighting flies in the face of conservation, where using smaller wattage bulbs, fluorescents, and the fewest number of light fixtures is the goal. I'm all for that when lighting your home on an everyday basis. But here, we're talking about a few weeks of showing your home. And chances are buyers will only be in your home a few hours of any given day, at most. Therefore, I beg forgiveness of those who are strong energy conservationists and simply make the case for an exception. You want to sell your home? You light up big time.

6. Change Wall and Window Coverings and Ceiling Appearance

The overall appearance of walls and ceilings count, too. How much they count is hard to say. My own feeling is that the most you can hope is for them to be neutral. In other words, I don't recall any buyer I've dealt with remarking about how wonderful the wall coverings or the ceiling looked. But, I've had many who commented on how bad they looked.

If you've got good wall coverings and ceilings, they won't detract from the appearance—they won't even be noticed. On the other hand, if there's something wrong with them, they can be distracting and cause a buyer to lower his or her estimation of your home. Thus, your job is to make the wall coverings and ceiling fade away from view so that buyers won't even notice them.

Walls

It should go without saying that if you have original or valuable pieces, you should store these safely before showing your home, for security reasons.

Beyond that it becomes a matter of taste. Perhaps yours runs to Salvador Dali or Modigliani, or some other artist whose works are dramatic in appearance. When it's you living in the home, copies of these on your walls may enhance your lifestyle. But, when you're showing your property to others, they may do just what you don't want—distract. You don't want potential buyers stopping to examine your pictures or what's worse, stopping to examine them and then deciding they don't like them. Your paintings have become anything but dispassionate.

When it comes to paintings, think of the boring hangings you might find in a hotel room. Typically, these are scenes of countrysides or villages without much color or drama in them. They're the sort of thing the eye passes over and barely notices. Yet, they provide an accent, a focal point, for the wall so it doesn't look bare. Perfect. That's what you want to emulate. (My apologies to art lovers who know good art and prefer to have it hanging on their walls. You're right, it does make a difference in your life. But, if you want a life in a new home, store it.)

Windows

Drapes/Curtains. Window treatments should be clean, in non-dramatic colors such as beige(!) or off-white, and hopefully not too outstanding in design. You want the drapes to cover windows or perhaps even a doorway. But, you don't want them to be overbearing. In one house I was recently viewing, the drapes throughout were a dark, forest green. Actually, they were a beautiful color. But, they darkened the rooms, and many buyers who came through didn't like the color. You could see the adding machine in those buyers' heads clicking away totaling up the dollars they'd deduct from the price they might offer because of the dark, green drapes they'd have to replace. Not a pleasant feeling for the sellers.

> **KEY CONCEPT** *With window and wall coverings, less tends to be more. If in doubt, leave the wall blank. If you can (as with windows at the back of the home) it's often more impressive to have no window coverings at all. Of course, this is awkward in bedrooms and in the front of the house, but where it works, try it. You may be surprised at how pleasant the "bare" look is.*

Shutters and Blinds. At one time, these were the ultimate window coverings for a home. Today, in many areas they are passé. This is not to say you should go to the expense of replacing them—don't. Just be aware that they may not bring the praise you hoped for.

If you do have shutters and/or blinds, be sure to have them cleaned. They collect dust easily and, if they haven't been cleaned in a few months, often have thick layers of it. A buyer passing his or her finger across them and coming up with a layer of dirt is a sure turn-off.

Also, be careful of the colors. Again, beige and off-white are fine. Anything else may need to be repainted to a nonoffensive color. (Repainting typically requires a pro to get it done right, although I've seen home owners with spray paint cans do remarkably good jobs.)

Shades. Leave them rolled up, unless they're necessary to keep the sunlight out of a buyer's eyes. While custom shades can be quite attractive, the old-fashioned yellow ones look, well, old-fashioned. The less seen of shades, usually the better.

Ceilings

Popcorn Ceilings. If you have these, you know it. These are "acoustical" ceilings that were very popular 30 and 40 years ago and are still present in many homes. A mixture of plaster and a bubbling agent were sprayed on the ceilings giving them a bumpy look. In some cases sparkles were added so that at night the ceiling was like a vast galaxy of stars. Unfortunately, today they are almost universally disliked.

My suggestion is that, if possible, you have these ceilings scraped, retextured, and repainted. The cost for a typical home of around 2,000 square feet is about $2,000—provided there is no asbestos in them (occurring mainly in homes built prior to 1978). If there is, the price jumps up dramatically, and they should be removed by an asbestos abatement company. (You can have your ceiling tested for asbestos by sending a small sample to a lab. Check *www.epa.gov/asbestos* for a listing of laboratories that test for asbestos.)

If you have popcorn ceilings, many buyers today will notice them and won't like them. They may subtract an unrealistically high price from any offer for removing the popcorn ceilings themselves. Or they may just figure it's too big a job to bother with and look for another house to buy.

If you decide not to remove the ceilings (or if it's too expensive because they contain asbestos), consider having them encapsulated and repainted. This is usually done by spraying first with a substance such as shellac, which tends to seal the ceilings, and then painting with a latex paint, which ends up giving them a nice, clean appearance. Again, use colors such as beige or off-white.

Ceiling Beams. Many older homes have ceiling beams as accents. If you have lots of wood in your home, they may work. But more often than not, they simply look old and dusty.

If the beams are strictly cosmetic (as many are), you can have them removed, the ceiling retextured as necessary, and repainted. Often the cost is only a few hundred dollars.

If they are structural and *if* it doesn't detract from the architectural design of your home, you may decide to paint them the same color as the ceiling. In this way, they'll blend in, be less noticeable, and not detract from the overall appearance of the room.

7. Deodorize

Smells are potent. Our noses, although nowhere nearly as sensitive as those of many animals, especially dogs, can quickly pick up odors, especially those that we identify as noxious. There's nothing that's going to turn a buyer off to a house quicker than to walk in and be accosted by a bad smell. I've opened the door to a home and immediately been hit by pet odors (some of the strongest) or mildew (frequently found in vacant homes) or other smells and simply didn't want to go inside.

All the rest of the home may be staged beautifully, but if it "stinks," it won't sell.

Here are some typical odors that occur in homes, their causes and some of their remedies:

- *Pets:* Most people love pets, including your author. However, they do have a slight body odor that can build up if a home is closed. Usually, just opening the windows and airing out the place will take of this.

  Much more serious is urine odor, the most pervasive of which comes from cats. If an animal has urinated on a carpet, you will need to replace the carpet, the padding, and in some cases the flooring beneath. After much experimenting with chemicals that claim to remove the odor, I've found that removal of the flooring is the only way that really works. Yes, it's expensive, but any buyer walking in and smelling the odor is likely to immediately depreciate the value of your home the inflated cost of new carpeting. Better you do it yourself at a more realistic cost.

  Additionally, many pet owners have a "pet room," sometimes a laundry room, where they keep a pet box. Even if the animal only uses this room, it will have an odor that will spread to other rooms.

  Therefore, though it may sound heartless, my suggestion is that you move your pet to a relative's or friend's home or even a kennel or vet during the (hopefully) short sales process, and then clean and remove any trace of odor.

  Please apologize to your pet for me . . . and you.

- *Mold and mildew:* In small quantities, these odors are hard to detect. But, if the house has been closed up for a few days, it's often quite noticeable. The mold and mildew can be quite clever in hiding from detection. Often it's underneath wall-to-wall carpeting. Most likely, it can be found in damp areas such as bathrooms, kitchen, and utility rooms.

  Remove any mold you find (if it's black mold, you may want to use a pest company to reduce any possibility of being injured by it; most termite companies can handle this for you). Once the mold is gone, air out the home and use a mild air freshener. Keeping the windows open for a few days should keep the smell from coming back.

A source of mold and mildew odor often overlooked is drains, especially the kitchen sink. Sometimes food sent down a garbage disposal or swept down a sink drain will not go all the way but instead will stick to the walls of the drain and rot. If you don't know where to look, the odor from this can be quite difficult to locate. Flushing the drain with water and a mild detergent often clears it right up.

- *Chemicals:* Chlorine bleaches, ammonia, and other household cleaners can leave an acrid smell that's quite annoying. Be sure to get rid of these and air the place out well before you show your home. Also, be wary of storing odorous chemicals, such as swimming pool chlorine, in your garage where their odors can waft into the home.

While removing unwanted odors is imperative, adding pleasant odors is an old agent's trick. I'm not talking about commercial fresheners, which have their own "cover-up" kind of odors. Rather, consider baking bread or biscuits in the oven when would-be buyers come by (and giving them a cookie!). Mulling cinnamon, apple cider, and spices on the stove is another trick to make your place more homey and appealing. Only don't overdo it—you want the pleasant odors as an accent, not something overpowering.

8. Add Flower Color

Adding flowers and trees can open the rooms of your home to the environment outside and add a soothing touch.

Try to use the color of flowers as accents, rather than as focal points. Often, dried flower arrangements or silk flowers make good choices as today's look almost better than the real thing and they require no maintenance. If you're going to use trees, get those with lots of green leaves (but be sure the leaves aren't falling off, lest they add a sense of decay to the home!). You'll want them in large pots as that helps them grow and also makes them look more native to the room.

Be careful of watering plants in pots: water that sloshes over the top or out the bottom can quickly stain flooring, especially carpeting. If it happens, thoroughly clean and dry immediately. Remove any stains. I find that Resolve works best on carpeting stains, but be sure to first test on a small piece of carpeting to be sure the remover doesn't add its own stain.

If you have any flowers, plants, or trees in the home that are dead or in the process of dying, remove them. Yes, you might be able to revive them with care over time. But right now you don't have the time. Get rid of them lest they make your home look dilapidated.

9. Change Furniture and Accessorize

Furniture

Consider this: take the large furniture pieces (sofas, overstuffed chairs, lounges) that you have in your living and family rooms and move them out. Store them away from the home or in an unused bedroom.

Now, in their place, take some furniture from your other rooms— small chairs, couches, and tables—and put these in your living room. Use colorful scarves, table covers, or other material to cover any that are worn. (Remember, it's all temporary, just for looks.)

Voilá. The small pieces will make your living areas look much bigger. And you've done it without spending any money. Very often sellers already have all the furniture they need to properly stage their home—all they need to do is to rearrange it.

Of course, it may not match. But in the eclectic world in which we live, that's not always terrible. Besides, if worst comes to pass, you can always buy inexpensive pieces to finish off a room. Consider plastic tables and chairs often used for outdoors or wicker furniture where you need inexpensive furniture quickly placed inside—slipcovers can make them look fashionable.

Where to Buy Inexpensive Furnishings for Staging

- Costco
- Cost Plus World Market
- Ikea
- Kmart
- Target
- Michael's
- Salvation Army
- Garage sales and other thrift stores

Another possibility is to rent it. There are many furniture rental companies available in nearly all cities. (Yes, it's expensive to do it on a long-term basis, but for a month or so, it's usually quite affordable.)

Large Furniture Rental Companies

- Rentfurniture.com
- Cort.com
- aaronrents.com
- Rent-A-Center

Accessorize

Adding pillows is a quick way to make a chair or couch look more comfortable, attractive, and colorful. Baskets near fireplaces can store small amounts of wood as well as magazines. Throw rugs strategically placed over heavily traveled areas as well as in hallways and entries can liven up a room.

Colorful placemats can turn a dingy dining room or kitchen table into one that's quite stylish. Cushions that can be tied to kitchen chairs can add softness and color to the room.

Don't forget sculptures, vases (even empty ones), and other knickknacks that provide accents to complement a room. Just be careful, as noted earlier; don't overdo it. You don't want your rooms to be bulging with too many little things.

10. Control Temperature and Noise

Watch the Temperature

Here's a trick I learned years ago and that most good sales-people know: people are most likely to make a purchase when the ambient temperature is a little under 70°F. Over 70 is too hot; under 68 is too cold.

No, making sure the temperature in your home is the magic 69 degrees is not going to guarantee the buyers will make an offer. But, it will create an environment where they will be likely to move forward toward a purchase, providing everything else (the home, their financing, and so on) also works.

Thus, if you're selling in the summertime, keep that air conditioning on. The power company is always telling you to raise the temperature of your air conditioning in summer to around 78 degrees to conserve energy—a wise thing to do. But, during those few weeks when your home is for sale, crank it down. When buyers come from a sizzling outdoors and find your home pleasantly cool, they'll want to stay there . . . perhaps permanently!

Similarly, in winter never mind about conserving energy during those weeks when your home is for sale. Crank it up to around 70. People coming in from the cold outside will likewise want to stay there. (Just be careful you don't make it too hot in winter. In cold weather regions, there's a tendency to make the inside too hot, and that as noted earlier, can be a turn-off in any weather.)

Watch Out for Noise

Part of buying a home is getting "quiet enjoyment." That means that buyers want their home to be quiet, not filled with distracting noises.

If your house is near a freeway (most people are surprised to learn just how loud freeway noise really is —typically about 80 decibels up to a quarter mile away), or there's a budding musician playing the drums in the afternoon down the street, or if airplanes fly low on a runway approach, try keeping your windows and doors closed when the home is shown. It's not that you're denying that there's noise, it's just that you're showing how quiet the home can be in spite of it. (If there's a serious noise problem, like a nearby airport, you'll want to disclose it to your buyers to help avoid liability problems after the sale.)

Another technique is to turn your stereo on low and play soothing music. Again, try to avoid such things as heavy metal and other music that's naturally loud or chaotic in sound. You're trying to create a bland atmosphere. No, it doesn't have to be elevator music, but on the other hand, you don't want it to draw attention away from your home.

And keep it turned down *low*. If a person has to raise his or her voice to be heard over the background music, it's up too loud.

8 Room-by-Room Checklist

BEING SELF-CRITICAL is probably one of the hardest things any of us can do. The same applies to our home. It can be a difficult stretch to gain objectivity when looking at rooms that we live in day in and day out.

But, to do a good job of staging that's just what you need to do. You need to get a "buyer's perspective" on your house. You need to see it through other people's eyes. And once you do that, you need to stage it in the most appealing way possible.

There are a number of ways you can gain external perspective (besides hiring an interior decorator or specialist in staging to come in and give you a paid-for opinion). Here are some tricks that I've found to be particularly helpful.

Tricks When Preparing to Stage a Room

- Think of where you stand after you enter a room. Usually, we seldom use all the corners of any room. We enter and then follow a beaten path (often reflected in traffic patterns in our carpet!) to a favorite chair, a counter, or whatever. But almost always there's a particular corner of the room that we almost never go into.

- Go into that corner now and look at the room as if you're seeing it for the first time. It should look different to you. For a few moments, you should be able to get a new perspective on it. This will help you see it as a stranger would. Now, ask yourself what would make it more appealing?

- When looking at the room, use your thumbs and index fingers to make a little box—and gaze through the box. (You've undoubtedly seen this parodied in movies where directors use it to frame scenes.) It actually helps eliminate distractions, and you'll be able to focus on the important parts of the room.

- Let your eyes wander around the room. Where do they land? That's the focus, the center of attention. Usually, it's a window or a piece of furniture. That's where you want to expend most of your energies.

- Go out of the room and turn around. Now peer back it through the open doorway from where you came. This is your line of sight into the room from other rooms. It's what other people will first see of the room. It may be the focal point or it may be another area. Remember, first impressions are important. What buyers first see should also bear special attention.

- Go back into the room and let its color, space, furnishings, and accessories wash over you. Now, is it as nice as you thought it was before you started this exercise? Or are there things you definitely need to change?

Staging Room by Room

As soon as you see what needs to be changed, you're ready to start staging. The following checklists will help you cover all the basics for each room in your house.

FIGURE 8.1 *Staging Checklists*

Entry

Walls

Neutral color?	☐	Clean all walls?	☐
Clean 1 wall?	☐	Repaint all walls?	☐
Repaint 1 wall?	☐	Scratches?	☐
Special work?	☐	Crayon marks?	☐

Ceiling

Neutral color?	☐	Repaint?	☐
Popcorn?	☐	Remove, plaster, paint?	☐
Beams?	☐	Remove?	☐
Clean, paint?	☐		

Floor

	Clean?	Replace?
Tile?	☐	☐
Wood?	☐	☐
Carpet?	☐	☐
Stone?	☐	☐
Other?	☐	☐

Lighting

Adequate?	☐
Poor?	☐
Excellent?	☐
Add bigger bulbs?	☐
Add new standing/table lamps?	☐
Add new fixtures?	☐

Furniture

Remove 1/3 to 1/2?	☐		
Rearrange?	☐	Swap with other rooms?	☐

	Store	Sell	Give Away	Buy New
Couch ?	☐	☐	☐	☐
Chair(s)?	☐	☐	☐	☐
Small table(s)?	☐	☐	☐	☐

Polish?	☐	Paint?	☐	Recover?	☐
Add scarf(s)?	☐	Add afghans?	☐	Add pillows?	☐

Additional Work

_____	☐	_____	☐

FIGURE 8.1 *Staging Checklists (continued)*

Living Room

Walls

Neutral color?	☐	Clean all walls?	☐
Clean 1 wall?	☐	Repaint all walls?	☐
Repaint 1 wall?	☐	Scratches?	☐
Special work?	☐	Crayon marks?	☐

Ceiling

Neutral color?	☐	Repaint?	☐
Popcorn?	☐	Remove, plaster, paint?	☐
Beams?	☐	Remove?	☐
Clean, paint?	☐		

Floor

	Clean?	Replace?
Tile?	☐	☐
Wood?	☐	☐
Carpet?	☐	☐
Stone?	☐	☐
Other?	☐	☐

Lighting

Adequate?	☐
Poor?	☐
Excellent?	☐
Add bigger bulbs?	☐
Add new standing/table lamps?	☐
Add new fixtures?	☐

Furniture

Remove 1/3 to 1/2?	☐		
Rearrange?	☐	Swap with other rooms?	☐

	Store	Sell	Give Away	Buy New
Couch ?	☐	☐	☐	☐
Chair(s)?	☐	☐	☐	☐
Small table(s)?	☐	☐	☐	☐

Polish?	☐	Paint?	☐	Recover?	☐
Add scarf(s)?	☐	Add afghans?	☐	Add pillows?	☐

Additional Work

_____ ☐   _____ ☐

FIGURE 8.1 *Staging Checklists (continued)*

Family Room

Walls

Neutral color?	☐	Repaint?	☐
Popcorn?	☐	Remove, plaster, paint?	☐
Beams?	☐	Remove?	☐
Clean, paint?	☐		

Ceiling

Neutral color?	☐	Repaint?	☐
Popcorn?	☐	Remove, plaster, paint?	☐
Beams?	☐	Remove?	☐
Clean, paint?	☐		

Floor

	Clean?	Replace?
Tile?	☐	☐
Wood?	☐	☐
Carpet?	☐	☐
Stone?	☐	☐
Other?	☐	☐

Lighting

Adequate?	☐
Poor?	☐
Excellent?	☐
Add bigger bulbs?	☐
Add new standing/table lamps?	☐
Add new fixtures?	☐

Furniture

Remove 1/3 to 1/2?	☐		
Rearrange?	☐	Swap with other rooms?	☐

	Store	Sell	Give Away	Buy New
Couch ?	☐	☐	☐	☐
Chair(s)?	☐	☐	☐	☐
Small table(s)?	☐	☐	☐	☐

Polish?	☐	Paint?	☐	Recover?	☐
Add scarf(s)?	☐	Add afghans?	☐	Add pillows?	☐

Entertainment Center

Clean?	☐	Polish	☐
Remove?	☐	Remove 1/3 to 1/2 of equipment?	☐

Additional Work

_____	☐	_____	☐

FIGURE 8.1 *Staging Checklists (continued)*

Dining Room

Walls

Neutral color?	☐	Clean all walls?	☐
Clean 1 wall?	☐	Repaint all walls?	☐
Repaint 1 wall?	☐	Scratches?	☐
Special work?	☐	Crayon marks?	☐

Ceiling

Neutral color?	☐	Repaint?	☐
Popcorn?	☐	Remove, plaster, paint?	☐
Beams?	☐	Remove?	☐
Clean, paint?	☐		

Floor

	Clean?	Replace?
Tile?	☐	☐
Wood?	☐	☐
Carpet?	☐	☐
Stone?	☐	☐
Other?	☐	☐

Lighting

Adequate?	☐
Poor?	☐
Excellent?	☐
Add bigger bulbs?	☐
Add new standing/table lamps?	☐
Add new fixtures?	☐

Furniture

Remove 1/3 to 1/2?	☐		
Rearrange?	☐	Swap with other rooms?	☐

	Store	Sell	Give Away	Buy New
Couch ?	☐	☐	☐	☐
Chair(s)?	☐	☐	☐	☐
Small table(s)?	☐	☐	☐	☐

Polish?	☐	Paint?	☐	Recover?	☐
Add scarf(s)?	☐	Add afghans?	☐	Add pillows?	☐

Additional Work

_____ ☐   _____ ☐

FIGURE 8.1 *Staging Checklists (continued)*

Kitchen

Walls

Neutral color?	☐	Clean all walls?	☐
Clean 1 wall?	☐	Repaint all walls?	☐
Repaint 1 wall?	☐	Scratches?	☐
Special work?	☐	Crayon marks?	☐

Ceiling

Neutral color?	☐	Repaint?	☐
Add track lights?	☐	Add recessed lights?	☐

Floor

	Clean?	Replace?
Tile?	☐	☐
Wood?	☐	☐
Linoleum?	☐	☐
Stone?	☐	☐
Other?	☐	☐

Lighting

Adequate?	☐
Poor?	☐
Excellent?	☐
Add bigger bulbs?	☐
Add new light fixtures?	☐

Appliances/Sink/Fixtures

Adequate?	☐
Poor?	☐
Excellent?	☐

	Clean?	Replace?
Stove?	☐	☐
Oven?	☐	☐
Dishwasher?	☐	☐
Oven Hood?	☐	☐
Compactor?	☐	☐
Microwave?	☐	☐
Garbage Disposal?	☐	☐
Kitchen Sink?	☐	☐
Faucet Assembly?	☐	☐
Other? _____	☐	☐
Other? _____	☐	☐

Additional Work

_____	☐	_____	☐

FIGURE 8.1 *Staging Checklists (continued)*

Master Bedroom

Walls

Neutral color?	☐	Clean all walls?	☐
Clean 1 wall?	☐	Repaint all walls?	☐
Repaint 1 wall?	☐	Scratches?	☐
Special work?	☐	Crayon marks?	☐

Ceiling

Neutral color?	☐	Repaint?	☐
Popcorn?	☐	Remove, plaster, paint?	☐
Beams?	☐	Remove?	☐
Clean, paint?	☐		

Floor

	Clean?	Replace?
Tile?	☐	☐
Wood?	☐	☐
Carpet?	☐	☐
Stone?	☐	☐
Other?	☐	☐

Lighting

Adequate?	☐
Poor?	☐
Excellent?	☐
Add bigger bulbs?	☐
Add new standing/table lamps?	☐
Add new fixtures?	☐

Furniture

Remove 1/3 to 1/2?	☐	Replace with smaller?	☐
Rearrange?	☐	Swap with other rooms?	☐

	Store	Sell	Give Away	Buy New
Bed?	☐	☐	☐	☐
Headboard?	☐	☐	☐	☐
Chair(s)?	☐	☐	☐	☐
Night stand(s)?	☐	☐	☐	☐

Polish?	☐	Paint?	☐	Recover?	☐
Add scarf(s)?	☐	Add afghans?	☐	Add pillows?	☐

Additional Work

_____	☐	_____	☐

FIGURE 8.1 *Staging Checklists (continued)*

Bedroom 2

Walls

Neutral color?	☐	Clean all walls?	☐
Clean 1 wall?	☐	Repaint all walls?	☐
Repaint 1 wall?	☐	Scratches?	☐
Special work?	☐	Crayon marks?	☐

Ceiling

Neutral color?	☐	Repaint?	☐
Popcorn?	☐	Remove, plaster, paint?	☐
Beams?	☐	Remove?	☐
Clean, paint?	☐		

Floor

	Clean?	Replace?
Tile?	☐	☐
Wood?	☐	☐
Carpet?	☐	☐
Stone?	☐	☐
Other?	☐	☐

Lighting

Adequate?	☐
Poor?	☐
Excellent?	☐
Add bigger bulbs?	☐
Add new standing/table lamps?	☐
Add new fixtures?	☐

Furniture

Remove 1/3 to 1/2?	☐	Replace with smaller?	☐
Rearrange?	☐	Swap with other rooms?	☐

	Store	Sell	Give Away	Buy New
Bed?	☐	☐	☐	☐
Headboard?	☐	☐	☐	☐
Chair(s)?	☐	☐	☐	☐
Night stand(s)?	☐	☐	☐	☐

Polish?	☐	Paint?	☐	Recover?	☐
Add scarf(s)?	☐	Add afghans?	☐	Add pillows?	☐

Additional Work

_____	☐	_____	☐

FIGURE 8.1 *Staging Checklists (continued)*

Bedroom 3

Walls

Neutral color?	☐	Clean all walls?	☐
Clean 1 wall?	☐	Repaint all walls?	☐
Repaint 1 wall?	☐	Scratches?	☐
Special work?	☐	Crayon marks?	☐

Ceiling

Neutral color?	☐	Repaint?	☐
Popcorn?	☐	Remove, plaster, paint?	☐
Beams?	☐	Remove?	☐
Clean, paint?	☐		

Floor

	Clean?	Replace?
Tile?	☐	☐
Wood?	☐	☐
Carpet?	☐	☐
Stone?	☐	☐
Other?	☐	☐

Lighting

Adequate?	☐
Poor?	☐
Excellent?	☐
Add bigger bulbs?	☐
Add new standing/table lamps?	☐
Add new fixtures?	☐

Furniture

Remove 1/3 to 1/2?	☐	Replace with smaller?	☐
Rearrange?	☐	Swap with other rooms?	☐

	Store	Sell	Give Away	Buy New
Bed?	☐	☐	☐	☐
Headboard?	☐	☐	☐	☐
Chair(s)?	☐	☐	☐	☐
Night stand(s)?	☐	☐	☐	☐

Polish?	☐	Paint?	☐	Recover?	☐
Add scarf(s)?	☐	Add afghans?	☐	Add pillows?	☐

Additional Work

_____	☐	_____	☐

FIGURE 8.1 *Staging Checklists (continued)*

Bedroom 4

Walls

Neutral color?	☐	Clean all walls?	☐
Clean 1 wall?	☐	Repaint all walls?	☐
Repaint 1 wall?	☐	Scratches?	☐
Special work?	☐	Crayon marks?	☐

Ceiling

Neutral color?	☐	Repaint?	☐
Popcorn?	☐	Remove, plaster, paint?	☐
Beams?	☐	Remove?	☐
Clean, paint?	☐		

Floor

	Clean?	Replace?
Tile?	☐	☐
Wood?	☐	☐
Carpet?	☐	☐
Stone?	☐	☐
Other?	☐	☐

Lighting

Adequate?	☐
Poor?	☐
Excellent?	☐
Add bigger bulbs?	☐
Add new standing/table lamps?	☐
Add new fixtures?	☐

Furniture

Remove 1/3 to 1/2?	☐	Replace with smaller?	☐
Rearrange?	☐	Swap with other rooms?	☐

	Store	Sell	Give Away	Buy New
Bed?	☐	☐	☐	☐
Headboard?	☐	☐	☐	☐
Chair(s)?	☐	☐	☐	☐
Night stand(s)?	☐	☐	☐	☐

Polish?	☐	Paint?	☐	Recover?	☐
Add scarf(s)?	☐	Add afghans?	☐	Add pillows?	☐

Additional Work

_____ ☐　　_____ ☐

FIGURE 8.1 *Staging Checklists (continued)*

Master Bathroom

Walls

Neutral color?	☐	Clean all walls?	☐
Clean 1 wall?	☐	Repaint all walls?	☐
Repaint 1 wall?	☐	Scratches?	☐
Special work?	☐	Crayon marks?	☐

Ceiling

Neutral color?	☐	Repaint?	☐
Add track lights?	☐	Add recessed lights?	☐

Floor

	Clean?	Replace?
Tile?	☐	☐
Wood?	☐	☐
Carpet?	☐	☐
Stone?	☐	☐
Llinoleum?	☐	☐
Other?	☐	☐

Lighting

Adequate?	☐
Poor?	☐
Excellent?	☐
Add bigger bulbs?	☐
Add new light fixtures?	☐

Fixtures

Adequate?	☐
Poor?	☐
Excellent?	☐

	Clean?	Replace?
Bathroom sink(s)?	☐	☐
Toilet?	☐	☐
Shower?	☐	☐
Tub?	☐	☐
Towel warmer?	☐	☐
Towel racks?	☐	☐
Faucets?	☐	☐
Other? _____	☐	☐

Additional Work

_____	☐	_____	☐

FIGURE 8.1 *Staging Checklists (continued)*

Guest Bathroom

Walls

Neutral color?	☐	Clean all walls?	☐
Clean 1 wall?	☐	Repaint all walls?	☐
Repaint 1 wall?	☐	Scratches?	☐
Special work?	☐	Crayon marks?	☐

Ceiling

Neutral color?	☐	Repaint?	☐
Add track lights?	☐	Add recessed lights?	☐

Floor

	Clean?	Replace?
Tile?	☐	☐
Wood?	☐	☐
Carpet?	☐	☐
Stone?	☐	☐
Llinoleum?	☐	☐
Other?	☐	☐

Lighting

Adequate?	☐
Poor?	☐
Excellent?	☐
Add bigger bulbs?	☐
Add new light fixtures?	☐

Fixtures

Adequate?	☐
Poor?	☐
Excellent?	☐

	Clean?	Replace?
Bathroom sink(s)?	☐	☐
Toilet?	☐	☐
Shower?	☐	☐
Tub?	☐	☐
Towel warmer?	☐	☐
Towel racks?	☐	☐
Faucets?	☐	☐
Other? _____	☐	☐

Additional Work

_____	☐	_____	☐

FIGURE 8.1 *Staging Checklists (continued)*

Utility Bathroom

Walls

Neutral color?	☐	Clean all walls?	☐
Clean 1 wall?	☐	Repaint all walls?	☐
Repaint 1 wall?	☐	Scratches?	☐
Special work?	☐	Crayon marks?	☐

Ceiling

Neutral color?	☐	Repaint?	☐
Add track lights?	☐	Add recessed lights?	☐

Floor

	Clean?	Replace?
Tile?	☐	☐
Wood?	☐	☐
Carpet?	☐	☐
Stone?	☐	☐
Llinoleum?	☐	☐
Other?	☐	☐

Lighting

Adequate?	☐
Poor?	☐
Excellent?	☐
Add bigger bulbs?	☐
Add new light fixtures?	☐

Fixtures

Adequate?	☐
Poor?	☐
Excellent?	☐

	Clean?	Replace?
Bathroom sink(s)?	☐	☐
Toilet?	☐	☐
Shower?	☐	☐
Tub?	☐	☐
Towel warmer?	☐	☐
Towel racks?	☐	☐
Faucets?	☐	☐
Other? _____	☐	☐

Additional Work

_____	☐	_____	☐

FIGURE 8.1 *Staging Checklists (continued)*

Hallways

Walls

Neutral color?	☐	Clean all walls?	☐
Clean 1 wall?	☐	Repaint all walls?	☐
Repaint 1 wall?	☐	Scratches?	☐
Special work?	☐	Crayon marks?	☐

Ceiling

Neutral color?	☐	Repaint?	☐
Popcorn?	☐	Remove, plaster, paint?	☐
Beams?	☐	Remove?	☐
Clean, paint?	☐		

Floor

	Clean?	Replace?
Tile?	☐	☐
Wood?	☐	☐
Carpet?	☐	☐
Stone?	☐	☐
Other?	☐	☐

Lighting

Adequate?	☐
Poor?	☐
Excellent?	☐
Add bigger bulbs?	☐
Add new standing/table lamps?	☐
Add new fixtures?	☐

Additional Work

_____	☐	_____	☐

Garage

Gear

Remove 1/3 to 1/2?	☐	Rearrange?	☐

	Store	Sell	Give Away	Buy New
Tools?	☐	☐	☐	☐
Boxes?	☐	☐	☐	☐
Furniture?	☐	☐	☐	☐
Other?	☐	☐	☐	☐

Additional Work

_____	☐	_____	☐

FIGURE 8.1 *Staging Checklists (continued)*

Finished Basement

Walls

Neutral color?	☐	Clean all walls?	☐
Clean 1 wall?	☐	Repaint all walls?	☐
Repaint 1 wall?	☐	Scratches?	☐
Special work?	☐	Crayon marks?	☐

Ceiling

Neutral color?	☐	Repaint?	☐
Popcorn?	☐	Remove, plaster, paint?	☐
Beams?	☐	Remove?	☐
Clean, paint?	☐		

Floor

	Clean?	Replace?
Tile?	☐	☐
Wood?	☐	☐
Carpet?	☐	☐
Stone?	☐	☐
Other?	☐	☐

Lighting

Adequate?	☐
Poor?	☐
Excellent?	☐
Add bigger bulbs?	☐
Add new standing/table lamps?	☐
Add new fixtures?	☐

Furnishings

Remove 1/3 to 1/2? ☐   Stuff? ☐   Rearrange? ☐

	Store	Sell	Give Away	Buy New
Tools?	☐	☐	☐	☐
Boxes?	☐	☐	☐	☐
Furniture?	☐	☐	☐	☐
Other?	☐	☐	☐	☐

Additional Work

_____ ☐   _____ ☐

FIGURE 8.1 *Staging Checklists (continued)*

Finished Attic

Walls

Neutral color?	☐	Clean all walls?	☐
Clean 1 wall?	☐	Repaint all walls?	☐
Repaint 1 wall?	☐	Scratches?	☐
Special work?	☐	Crayon marks?	☐

Ceiling

Neutral color?	☐	Repaint?	☐
Popcorn?	☐	Remove, plaster, paint?	☐
Beams?	☐	Remove?	☐
Clean, paint?	☐		

Floor

	Clean?	Replace?
Tile?	☐	☐
Wood?	☐	☐
Carpet?	☐	☐
Stone?	☐	☐
Other?	☐	☐

Lighting

Adequate?	☐
Poor?	☐
Excellent?	☐
Add bigger bulbs?	☐
Add new standing/table lamps?	☐
Add new fixtures?	☐

Furnishings

Remove 1/3 to 1/2? ☐   Stuff? ☐   Rearrange? ☐

	Store	Sell	Give Away	Buy New
Tools?	☐	☐	☐	☐
Boxes?	☐	☐	☐	☐
Furniture?	☐	☐	☐	☐
Other?	☐	☐	☐	☐

Additional Work

_____ ☐   _____ ☐

9 Staging When Your Home Is Vacant

HOW DO YOU prepare a home to show when you're no longer living in it?

You may have changed jobs and moved to another region of the country. Or you've already bought another home and moved into it. Or you had a sale that fell through and now you have to resell your vacant home. Or . . . ? There are countless reasons your home may be empty. If it is, you should be aware that staging it requires special attention.

Problems with Staging Vacant Homes

Vacant homes present special problems:

- No one's there to turn on all the lights and bake cookies (create wholesome, enticing odors) in the oven or otherwise get the home ready to show.

- Often the furniture is gone (moved to your next home) leaving the house barren. It's a common fact in real estate that homes empty of all furniture are harder to sell than those occupied (with furniture).

- Vacant homes tend to be cold in winter and hot in summer as the sellers turn down the heat and air to save costs. Hence, buyers find the places unwelcoming.

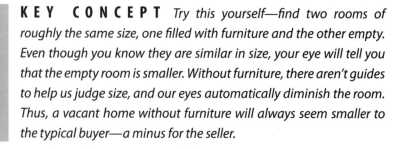

K E Y   C O N C E P T *Try this yourself—find two rooms of roughly the same size, one filled with furniture and the other empty. Even though you know they are similar in size, your eye will tell you that the empty room is smaller. Without furniture, there aren't guides to help us judge size, and our eyes automatically diminish the room. Thus, a vacant home without furniture will always seem smaller to the typical buyer—a minus for the seller.*

How to Stage a Vacant Home

The first step is to realize this is a special situation that requires extra attention. Simply moving out of your home and expecting it to be just as easy to sell as when you were in it won't work. You have to jump through a few extra hoops if you expect to get a quick sale and a good price.

1. Clean Out All Clutter

When most of us move, we tend to leave lots of stuff behind. Most common are boxes that are filled with items to be thrown or given away. Often, there are cords from TVs, ironing boards that are bent and don't work, broken chairs, and so on. We're leaving, so we leave what we don't want or need.

This simply won't do. Go back and clean *all clutter* out of the home. There should be nothing left on the floors in any room (other than some furniture, as discussed later). And don't simply move it into a corner of the room or stack it in a closet—remove it from the property. It has to go anyhow, so why not get rid of it immediately?

2. Pay Special Attention to Cleaning

Whenever you move your furniture out of a home, you'll find scratches on the walls and floors that were previously hidden by your things. Thus, after you take out your furniture you'll need to go back and wash, clean, and repaint.

This is both good and bad. The bad part is that it's extra work for you. The good part is that without furniture in the property it's easier to do.

Pay special attention to any marks on the walls and carpets. Without furniture in the home, these will tend to stand out. Get the carpets thoroughly cleaned. Or, if that doesn't work, consider having them replaced. Clean or repaint the walls. (Do the whole wall on which the mark occurs so as not to leave clean and dirty areas.)

Broom clean, wash, and then polish any linoleum floors. Polish wood floors. Thoroughly clean any tile or stone floors.

3. Consider Leaving Some Furniture

Yes, this is definitely going to be inconvenient. (It could mean two moves: a big one and then a later small one.) However, it should be worthwhile.

When you move out, don't take all of your furniture with you. Instead leave a few pieces. For example, leave a couple of chairs and a coffee table in the living room and perhaps a small couch with end tables in the family or den. Leave a bed (at least a double but preferably a queen) with nightstands in the master bedroom. If you have an eating area in the kitchen, leave a small kitchen table with two chairs. And leave a chair or table in other rooms as well.

Do the same with wall hangings. Leave drapes, curtains, and other window coverings. If you have pictures on the wall that you obtained for staging purposes (see Chapter 7), leave them hanging.

The whole idea is that when buyers come through the home, they'll have guides to size. They'll see the rooms as bigger than if they were completely empty.

4. Rent Some Furniture

If, for whatever reason, you can't leave some of your own furniture, seriously consider renting some. As noted in Chapter 7, you can almost always rent furniture from a variety of sources. Get some nice pieces, especially for the living areas and the master bedroom.

Renting furniture has an advantage over leaving your own in that you may not have to move twice. If you get the rental company to deliver and pick up, you won't have to worry about double moving. And in many cases, you should be able to choose better pieces to fit your rooms than your own!

5. Be Sure the Yard Is Kept Up

Nothing will ruin your sale faster than losing curb appeal by having your yard run down. And this is easy to have happen when you're not living there.

My suggestion is that you utilize a gardener, unless you want to come by and take care of it yourself. Presuming you've already fixed it up and staged it (see Chapters 5 and 7), you need to be sure that everything is always watered, the lawn mowed at least once a week, the shrubs trimmed, and so forth. You can't let the yard go just because you're not around and still expect a quick sale for a good price.

6. Use Flowers and Greenery Inside

We've already discussed flower-power in Chapter 7. What we said there holds true whether or not your home is vacant. Indeed, adding flowers can help fill out a room when there's little furniture in it. Look particularly for small indoor trees in larger pots. You probably won't want them in all but the major rooms and only one to a room, but they will help.

In the kitchen and bathrooms consider using flowering plants. Cut flowers are an option, but since you're not there to tend to them, you're probably better off with potted plants or artificial flowers.

A word of caution—don't overdo it with flowers and indoor greenery in a vacant home. Too much can quickly be distracting making the place look too much like a greenhouse. Remember, less can be more, in this case.

KEY CONCEPT *The rooms to keep a small amount of furniture in are:*

- *Living room*
- *Dining room*
- *Family room/den*
- *Master bedroom*
- *Kitchen*

If you don't have furniture in other bedrooms, hallway, entry, and other areas, don't worry about it. It's the important rooms that count most.

Use an Agent

In Chapter 13 we'll discuss the possibility of selling your home FSBO (by owner). If you sell it yourself you can have better control over the sale, and you should save money on the commission you'd otherwise pay.

However, if your home is vacant, I suggest you'd be better off using an agent. You should find that even though it could be more expensive, it's also quicker and easier.

Convenience

As an FSBO, when you're living in the home, it's easy as pie to show it to prospective buyers. You simply arrange a time. You're there anyhow, so it's just a matter of opening the door and walking them through.

On the other hand, if you're not living there, it's another matter. You have to stop whatever you're doing and run down to the house to open it up. Because buyers frequently want to come by during the day, that could be very inconvenient, particularly if you're working. You'd have to take time off from your regular job to show your home—something you might not want or be able to do.

More Showing Time

When your home is filled with furniture, it takes a while for potential buyers to walk through. They tend to stop in each room and size it up, figuring how big it is, its condition, where their furniture would go, and so on. When your home is vacant, the walk-through can take a few seconds. After all, there's little to see except mostly empty rooms. (Hopefully, you've left or added some furniture!)

However, an agent can slow down the process. It's much easier for an agent, who already has the confidence of the buyers, to point out where their couch and end tables could go; how well their dining room table would fit; the direction their king-sized bed would face.

Association

Finally, when you show a vacant house, you'll find that the buyers have trouble associating you with the property. After all, you live somewhere else. Yet, you're not an agent. Are you an investor? Are you a real estate pro trying to pull the wool over their eyes?

As a seller-occupant you have a certain credibility. As a nonoccupant owner, you tend to lose that. You have to spend more time selling yourself, explaining why you moved out and why the home is vacant.

In short, with a vacant home it's always easier and usually quicker to use an agent.

Make Special Arrangements for Showing

Finally, even if you are using an agent, you should make special arrangements for showing the property. For example, there's the matter of making sure that all the lights are on. When you're living there, you simply turn them on as soon as the agent calls to tell you he or she's coming by with a prospective buyer. What do you do if you don't live there?

My suggestion is that you make special arrangements with a trusted neighbor. That person can come over and turn on the lights before the property is shown.

Don't count on the agent to handle the lighting for you. Agents seldom come by to stage the house before they bring the buyer. Yes, they can move room to room turning on and turning off lights as they show the property, but it's awkward, and many don't do a good job of it.

If you're really willing go the whole nine yards in getting a quicker sale, my suggestion is that each morning you drop by and turn on the lights. Then drop by later in the day and turn them off. At the same time, you can turn up the heating and cooling and later turn it down. Yes, it's going to drive up your utility bills. But, if it's only for a few weeks and if gets a quicker sale at a better price, it's well worth the cost.

As far as keeping something going on the stove to create pleasant odors, it's probably not a good idea. If you can't watch it, it might burn, creating some really bad odors (or in the worst case, start a fire).

Another alternative is to buy a lot of those small controls that fit between the wall plug and lights. (Often several light fixtures can be run from one controller.) They can be set to go on and off a specific times—some do it automatically, attuned to outdoor lighting. And digital thermostats can accomplish the same thing. Of course, it's another expense if you don't have them, one that can be avoided if you can manage to come by the home several times a day yourself.

Note: It's probably not a good idea to simply leave the lights on all night and day. It might disturb your neighbors and could alert those with malicious intent that your home is vacant.

Condo—a Special Case

If your home is in a condominium development, especially if it's gated, you may find that showing is more difficult when the property is vacant. Often the development will not allow unescorted guests (potential buyers) in. Further, finding your unit in a large group can sometimes be more difficult for buyers. An agent here is indispensable.

On the other hand, with so many neighbors nearby and sometimes with homeowner's association staff nearby, you may be able to work out an arrangement for turning on lights and controlling temperature, even if it costs you a few bucks a week.

Janet's Sale

A friend of mine, Janet, was selling her home and because of a job change, had to quickly move out of state. She had to be at her new job even before she had finished staging her home and putting it up for sale.

She quickly went through the fix-up steps outlined in Chapters 1 through 5, then moved on to staging. She didn't have a lot of time to make decisions, so she acted smartly and quickly.

She needed her furniture and because it was a long-distance move, she didn't want to move twice. So she moved everything she had out of her home and onto a van for transport to her new apartment.

Then she hired a crew to come in and remove any clutter remaining as well as do a thorough cleaning of the home. The cost was only a few hundred dollars. For $1,200 more she hired a painter to quickly come in and paint the living room, dining room, family room, kitchen, and master bedroom (but not the ceilings which were in good shape). Because her carpeting was fairly new, she just had it thoroughly cleaned, and it came out looking great. She also took care of cleaning out her attic and garage, especially removing any remaining storage boxes.

In short, within two and half weeks, Janet's home was in sparkling condition. She then hired an agent to handle the sale. The agent had a teenaged son, and she made a special arrangement with him. Before school and then in the evening he would come by and turn on and off all the lights. He'd also check the temperature, make sure plants were watered, and generally watch out for the house. Mom, the agent, promised to keep an eye on the son, and Janet thought this a fine arrangement. For it, she paid him $25 a week. (She already had a gardener who took care of the exterior for her.)

The agent was diligent and the house sold within three weeks. Janet never had to come back. Everything was handled long distance. A perfect result for her, demonstrating how a vacant home can be staged and sold just as quickly as an occupied house.

10 From "House Wreck" to "House Beautiful"

I'VE OFTEN BEEN asked, "What are the most important things I can do to stage my home?" While all of the items we've covered in this section are important, here are the top three, along with case histories of people who have had personal, and sometime painful, experiences with them.

Clean, Color, Declutter

If you do nothing else, these three are critical to the staging of your home. The reason? Simple; they'll make the most difference to buyers.

Remember, it's not you that you're trying to please when you stage your home. It's a variety of buyers. You want to hit the broadest range possible, and that means creating a home environment that's spotlessly clean (no matter the price of your home), is neutral colored, and decluttered to the point where buyers can see how their things will fit. Hit all three and you've turned your home into a winner.

Clean, Clean, Clean

Roger and Jasmine owned an unremarkable 3-bedroom, 3-bath home in a suburb of Phoenix, Arizona. They had lived there for three years. When they moved in, the homes were only a year old and the neighborhood was quiet. But in the intervening years, lots of families with teenagers had moved in, and now there were occasional problems at night—some rowdiness and drunkenness and occasionally a fight. The neighborhood was still pleasant enough to look at. But Roger and Jasmine feared that in a few more years gangs could become involved and that could adversely affect housing prices, not to mention a quiet lifestyle. So, they decided to sell and move to what they hoped would be a better neighborhood.

Jasmine and Roger considered themselves to be fairly good housekeepers and assumed that their house was neat and clean. They figured that they wouldn't have to do any special work to get it ready. In other words, they didn't plan on doing any staging.

The first thing they did was hire an agent and put the home up for sale. They asked just a little bit higher than the highest price previously received in their neighborhood.

The house had many agents come by during the first two weeks. (The best time to attract interest in a home from agents is when it's first listed—see Chapter 9.) Jasmine's and Roger's agent, Rosa, talked to many of these agents and universally they said they wouldn't show the property because it was so dirty. There were water stains in tubs and in the toilet bowls, the counters weren't clean, and the windows were dirty. Rosa approached Roger and Jasmine on the subject in a diplomatic way, telling them what other agents had commented on. The couple listened and then pooh-poohed the comments. They were quite sure that their home was in fine condition.

So Rosa said that she'd like to try something. Her office was offering a new staging service. It was essentially free to Jasmine and Roger. She would send a cleaning crew around. They told Rosa it wasn't necessary, but since it was a free service, why not try it?

Rosa's crew came out and washed and cleaned everything. They got rid of the grime and stains in the tubs, toilets, and sinks; washed the windows; cleaned the floors; and in general made the place look clean as a whistle. The cost was $250, which Rosa paid out of her own pocket.

The home had now been for sale for a month, and most of the agents who had seen it in its previous condition decided it was a fixer and didn't show it. Rosa had her work cut out convincing agents to come back for a second look.

It was a few more weeks before agents began drifting back. Unfortunately, by then Roger's and Jasmine's home began drifting back to its old condition. They didn't maintain the level of cleanliness that Rosa had paid the cleaning crew to establish.

The home languished until a week before the listing was ready to expire. Then a "bottom fisher" (a buyer looking to "steal" a property) came in with a low offer. By then Roger and Jasmine were desperate. They countered, but when the buyer wouldn't up his offer, they accepted the original low bid.

The moral here is that while cleanliness may or may not be next to godliness, it certainly is next to sellingness. If you want to sell your home quickly and for a good price, clean, clean, clean! It's the most basic thing you can do to stage a property.

Colorize

Sal (short for Sally) owned a medium-sized, 3-bedroom, 2-bath condo. Her husband had died within the past year, and now she wanted to move to a smaller home. Also, she wanted to get away from the memories of the house they had shared. She decided to sell.

Sal cleaned her home thoroughly until it was spotless. No one could fault for her having a dirty place. She had passed the most basic test of staging.

However, during their ownership, Sal and her husband had painted the home to suit their own tastes. They liked what they called "earth" colors. These included forest green ceilings and walls that were yellow, brown, or red. The study, which was the first room you saw when entering the house, she painted a deep burgundy color. They offset these strong solid colors with complementary furniture that had colorful floral patterns. To Sal and her husband, the home sang of life, color, and beauty.

Unfortunately, to agents who came by it tended to look like a circus of color. There wasn't an agent whom Sal interviewed who didn't tell her that the colors would offend buyers and that she should have the place repainted.

Perhaps if her husband had been alive, Sal might have resisted the suggestions. But, she wanted to sell and assumed that since all of the agents agreed on this one point, it must be true. So for $2,100 she hired a painter to come and paint out the entire house in a light beige. He had to go over it twice to cover the darker colors on the walls.

Sal said the new colors made the place look like a hotel lobby, not at all homey. The agents disagreed and now commented on her floral furniture. They said it should be removed, or at least most of the brightest pieces taken out.

Again Sal complied. She held the property off the market for two weeks while this was all done, and then put it up for sale—staged to show. It sold within three days at her asking price.

The moral is that colorizing pays. Remember, the colors that make your home perfect for you may offend many buyers in the range you hope to attract. Neutralizing color helps sell your home, even if it makes it less "homey."

Declutter

Jerry lived alone in a 5-bedroom, 4-bathroom house that he had inherited from his parents when they were tragically killed in an automobile accident six years earlier. He never moved into the master bedroom, but instead stayed in a large side bedroom that he had occupied before he inherited the home.

Jerry was a collector. He was both a numismatist (collected rare coins) as well as a philatelist (collected rare stamps). In addition, he subscribed to a local newspaper as well as the *New York Times,* the *Economist,* the *London Times,* as well as other newspapers and magazines from around the world. He felt these gave him a broad perspective on world events, and he saved all the issues for reference (although he himself admitted he rarely went back to look at them).

Jerry's home, thus, was filled with boxes and boxes of old newspapers and magazines. In addition, the old furniture in all the bedrooms and living areas that he inherited from his parents had been converted to storage space. He kept posters and knickknacks there, accumulated from his travels (he had toured Europe and Asia).

One day Jerry decided that he wanted to live in France. So, he called an agent to list his home. He would sell it for a good price, considering how much it had gone up in value the last few years, and live off the proceeds. He figured if spent wisely, the money could last him at least 10 years. Of course, he wanted to get as much as possible from the sale.

The agent was thrilled to get the listing as the home was in a highly desirable area. She did a thorough CMA (comparative market analysis—see Chapter 11) and put the home on the market for $980,000. She told Jerry he had a week to get rid of all the clutter before the house came out on the MLS (Multiple Listing Service). Jerry replied, "What clutter?"

It was only then that the agent realized the extent of the problem she faced. Buyers would surely see the house as so cluttered as to be unlivable. She didn't think any agent worth his or her salt would show without explaining that it was a fixer. And that meant nose-diving the price.

So, she offered to send a crew out to move all of the clutter into a Clementina—a large metal garbage bin that the garbage company would put on the street. Jerry refused. He said he could not throw away anything. It was valued reference material.

She then offered to have the crew put it in boxes and stored away. Again Jerry refused. He said he would pack it all carefully himself over time. And then he'd have it shipped to Lyon, France, where he planned to move. He planned to pack it up over the next few weeks and months.

The agent couldn't move him. So the home sat there. Three months later when the listing expired, Jerry still hadn't packed up more than one of the bedroom's worth of clutter.

Jerry relisted with a different agent and the home again sat for three months without selling. During that time, some bottom fishers made low-ball offers, but Jerry refused. He said he wouldn't sell until he got his price.

Two years and four other listers later, Jerry finally did sell his property—for full price. He had by then packed up roughly half his stuff and asked for a long escrow to pack the remainder.

Jerry felt satisfied because he had gotten his price. However, during those two years the prices for homes in his area had appreciated 15 percent and 17 percent per year. Jerry had actually sold for more than 30 percent below market at the time of the sale because of high housing inflation at the time.

The moral here is, obviously, declutter your home. Jerry probably would have gotten full price and a quick sale two years earlier *if* he had taken his agent's advice. Or two years later he might very well have gotten 30+ percent more *if* the home was decluttered.

Obviously there are few Jerrys out there. His is an extreme example. But, all of us have some clutter. And even if it's a very small amount, it will hold up the sale and adversely affect the price.

The "3 Cs"

Clean, color, and declutter: These are the most basic staging strategies for staging your house. If you do nothing else, do these. And you will greatly improve your chances for a quick sale at a good price.

PART THREE

Sell It!

11 Price It to Sell Quick!

IT'S A GOOD idea to keep your eye on your target. And the bull's eye for you is getting a good price on a quick sale. Now that your home is fixed up and properly staged, it's time to make that happen.

Why the Price Needs to Be Right

Almost any agent will tell you, "Lower the price to get a quick sale." That's true, but you're looking to get that quick sale at a *good price*. That, after all, is why you fixed up and staged the property. You want the *optimum* price in a quick sale. If you were simply going to give the property away, why bother fixing it up and staging it?

To get that top price, and quickly, we have to return to what we talked about in earlier chapters as "visual value." The buyer has to be able to see that the price is justified by what you're offering. That means that the price has to be right for the home in the condition you've put it in. It can't be too high, else the buyer will readily see that you've overpriced your home . . . and move on. Or too low, in which case you'll be leaving "money on the table" when you sell.

How does the buyer make that visual value judgment?

The answer is the same way that you do, by checking out the competition.

Let's look at it from the buyer's perspective for a moment. You have to assume that in today's market you're dealing with a savvy buyer. This isn't someone who just fell off a turnip truck.

Your assumption should be that your buyer has seen (or soon will see) everything else that's available. If that's true, then your buyer is able to make an intelligent comparison—your house against all the others.

KEY CONCEPT *No matter what your price or how well you've fixed and staged your home, chances are you will get a few low-ball offers. There are always bottom-feeders looking to "steal" a property. They make low-ball offers on dozens of homes, hoping that at least one will get accepted. When you get a low-ball, don't despair or throw in the towel. Just accept it as a way of life when selling property and move on. Of course, I always counter a low-ball offer with a high-ball one. You never know—sometimes that low-baller will fall in love with your fixed and staged property and turn around to pay top dollar for it!*

Presumably, because of the fixing and staging work you've done, your home should look better than any of the others. That means that in a head-to-head comparison, your home should take top dollar. In a range of prices, your home should be right there at the pinnacle. The "visual value" should be obvious. And that will be reflected in the buyer's offer.

On the other hand, no matter how well you've fixed and staged your home, don't expect to get more than the top of the price range for your neighborhood. Yes, you might actually get the highest price ever for a comparable home. But, you're not going to get a million dollars for a hundred-thousand-dollar house. And you're wasting your time if you try.

If you overprice your home beyond the range of the comps, beyond the range of homes in your neighborhood, a buyer will simply pass. He or she will move up to a house in a better neighborhood. Remember, you're not only in competition with all the comps in your own neighborhood, but you're also in competition with all the other neighborhoods in your region.

Thus, your goal is just the right price: high enough to be warranted by your home's visual value, but not so high as to drive buyers away.

Homes Sold versus Homes for Sale

Your main guide to pricing should be what comparable homes have actually sold for. That should establish the basic range of prices charged for homes in your area. (Also check out Chapter 3 for more information on comps.)

However, the price of homes previously sold is a reference to the past. It doesn't take into account today's price trends (whether moving upward or downward), nor the size of today's inventory, nor the condition of comparable houses currently for sale but not yet sold.

> **K E Y   C O N C E P T** *Some sellers tell themselves that it can't hurt to overprice their home. A savvy buyer can always make a more realistic offer, while by overpricing they hope that a one-in-a-million fool will actually pay their price. Not so. Savvy buyers tend not to make any offers on overpriced properties. They see such sellers as foolish and stubborn and more trouble than they're worth.*

Thus, my suggestion is that after you've determined the price range of comps based on previous sales and seen where your home fits in, you now compare your home to its immediate competitors: other homes in your area also for sale. This will help you refine your price upward or downward based on what's available today to buyers. (But, always keep in mind that comps of homes sold is a far more solid reference than comps of homes for sale but not yet sold.)

Getting to That Right Price

For the remainder of this chapter we're going to focus in on how to hit the optimum target price for your home. That's the highest price that will get a sale, quick!

So let's get started: If you haven't already done so, get a list of comparable sales going back at least six months. Also, get a list of comparable homes that are currently for sale in your neighborhood. These lists should include as complete a description of the comps as possible.

You can get all of this information from a variety of sources. Most of it you can usually get simply online by going to websites such as:

- *http://realestate.yahoo.com/*
- *www.zillow.com*
- *www.dataquick.com*

These and other sites contain information on recent sales of homes. Despite the fact that they are national in scope, they often contain amazingly detailed information on local sales in most areas. Of course, if your home is not in a tract, but rather custom built, you'll have to do some extrapolation.

Another good source is a local real estate agent. In Chapter 13 we're going to talk about hiring the optimum agent. One of the things you can ask agents who apply for the job is to provide you with a thorough CMA (comparable market analysis). Almost any agent will do this for you free in the hope that you'll select them for the listing.

This should offer you a detailed description of all the comparable homes that have sold within the past six months. If you ask for it, you should also be supplied with a detailed description of all comparable homes that are currently for sale.

Use the list of actual sales to determine the price range for homes in your neighborhood. Use the list of homes currently for sale, but unsold, to tell you how many homes are for sale in your specific area (inventory), whether prices are trending up or down, and what the competition looks like.

K E Y   C O N C E P T *Agents can almost always arrange to show you comparable homes currently "for sale" that compete with yours. Check out the competition. See how your home fits in terms of location, price, fixed-up and staged condition, and features. If there's something out there much better than yours selling for less than you planned on listing your home for, it might suggest you're aiming too high. On the other hand, if everything else out there is junk, maybe you're aiming too low!*

The Comp Sheets

For each comp home (both sold and currently for sale), fill out a comp report sheet like those shown in this chapter. Remember, you should be able to get most of the information from old or current listings provided to you by an agent. However, you may find it harder to get information on the condition of sold homes without actually driving by them. Also, you can flavor the reports by what you personally see when you visit each currently "for sale" property. (Note: You'll want to make extra copies of these comp sheets so you'll have enough for each home that you compare.)

FIGURE 11.1 *Comp Sheets*

Comp Sheet for Comparable Home Currently for Sale

Price? _____

Special terms* (if known)? _____

Location?_____

School district? _____

Curb appeal†? _____

Age? _____

Style? _____

Lot size? _____

Corner/flag lot (subtract value)? _____

Square footage of home?§ _____

Stories? _____

Bedrooms? _____

Bathrooms? _____

Condition of kitchen? _____

Condition of master bedroom? _____

Condition of master bathroom? _____

Condition of exterior of home? _____

Overall condition of interior? _____

Colorization? _____

Furniture appeal? _____

Lighting appeal? _____

Decluttering? _____

Condition of yard? _____

Pool? _____

Spa? _____

Fireplace? _____

Community park? _____

Other amenity (tennis or basketball court, for example)? _____

Upgraded roof? _____

Upgraded windows? _____

Upgraded flooring? _____

Systems adequate and working:

    Heating/cooling? _____

    Electrical? _____

    Plumbing? _____

FIGURE 11.1 *Comp Sheets (continued)*

Comp Sheet for Comparable Home Sold Recently

Sold when? _____ (Try to keep within the last 6 months)
Price? _____
Special terms* (if known)? _____
Location?_____
School district? _____
Curb appeal†? _____
Age? _____
Style?_____
Lot size?_____
Stories? _____
Corner/flag lot (subtract value)? _____
Square footage of home?§ _____
Bedrooms? _____
Bathrooms?_____
Condition of yard? _____
Pool? _____
Spa?_____
Fireplace? _____
Community park?_____
Other amenity (tennis or basketball court, for example)? _____
Condo/co-op/townhouse/detached single family? _____

If Information Is Available
Condition of kitchen?_____
Condition of master bedroom? _____
Condition of master bathroom? _____
Condition of exterior of home? _____
Overall condition of interior?_____
Colorization?_____
Furniture appeal? _____
Lighting appeal?_____
Decluttering? _____
Upgraded roof? _____
Upgraded windows? _____
Upgraded flooring? _____
Systems adequate and working:
    Heating/cooling? _____
    Electrical? _____
    Plumbing?_____

FIGURE 11.1 *Comp Sheets (continued)*

Comp Sheet for Your Home

Price?_____

Special terms?_____

Location?_____

School district? _____

Curb appeal?_____

Age? _____

Style?_____

Lot size?_____

Stories? _____

Corner/flag lot (subtract value)? _____

Square footage of home?_____

Bedrooms? _____

Bathrooms?_____

Condition of kitchen?_____

Condition of master bedroom? _____

Condition of master bathroom? _____

Condition of exterior of home? _____

Overall condition of interior?_____

Condition of yard? _____

Pool? _____

Fireplace? _____

Community park?_____

Spa?_____

Other amenity (tennis or basketball court, for example)? _____

Upgraded roof? _____

Upgraded windows? _____

Upgraded flooring? _____

Systems adequate and working:

    Heating/cooling? _____

    Electrical? _____

    Plumbing?_____

* Sometimes the price can be artificially high or low because of terms agreed upon between buyer and seller. For example, the seller may be carrying back a low-interest-rate second mortgage, thus boosting the price. Or, the buyer may have agreed to a short escrow and a cash purchase, thus lowering the price.

† You can usually check this out by just driving by the home in question.

§ Some buyers and sellers mistakenly judge property on the basis of square footage: the home is selling for $100 or $350 a square foot or whatever. This is only applicable for homes in the same location. It's inappropriate for homes in different locations. Remember, in real estate the single most important factor in pricing is location, not the size of the home on the lot.

Making the Comparison

Once you've filled out your comp sheets, you can make the comparison to come up with your correct price. The master sheet shown in Figure 11.2 should prove helpful.

Understanding Special Factors That Affect Pricing

Although not always mentioned specifically by the comp sheets, the following factors affect the pricing of all homes in an area. How you finesse them could mean more or less money for you.

School District

You should never underestimate the importance of local schools to the value of your home (see comp sheets). Many buyers shop school districts before anything else. It's a rule in real estate that the better the schools in an area, the more people will want to live there and, hence, the higher the prices sellers can command.

This should already be built into the price of comparables and homes currently for sale. And if yours is a good school district, that's a good thing to point out to prospective buyers, particularly if you're asking the top of your range.

You should make it a point to learn about your local schools. All school districts use some sort of testing to determine the percentile rank of their students within the state and often within the country. These ranking should be readily available from local schools boards. Find them out for your area and, particularly if they are high, have them available for a buyer's perusal. It could be an easy way to score a quick sale.

Market Trends

Sometimes the residential real estate market is trending up. Sometimes it's trending down. And sometimes it just sort of sits there moving sideways.

FIGURE 11.2 *Master Comparison Sheet*

Master Comparison Sheet

	Yours #1	#2	#3	#4	#5	#6	#7
Price?	___	___	___	___	___	___	___
Special terms?	___	___	___	___	___	___	___
Location?	___	___	___	___	___	___	___
School district?	___	___	___	___	___	___	___
Curb appeal?	___	___	___	___	___	___	___
Age?	___	___	___	___	___	___	___
Style?	___	___	___	___	___	___	___
Lot size?	___	___	___	___	___	___	___
Stories?	___	___	___	___	___	___	___
Corner/flag lot?	___	___	___	___	___	___	___
Square footage?	___	___	___	___	___	___	___
Bedrooms?	___	___	___	___	___	___	___
Bathrooms?	___	___	___	___	___	___	___
Condition of kitchen?	___	___	___	___	___	___	___
Condition of master bedroom?	___	___	___	___	___	___	___
Condition of master bathroom?	___	___	___	___	___	___	___
Condition of exterior?	___	___	___	___	___	___	___
Overall condition?	___	___	___	___	___	___	___
Condition of yard?	___	___	___	___	___	___	___
Pool?	___	___	___	___	___	___	___
Fireplace?	___	___	___	___	___	___	___
Community park?	___	___	___	___	___	___	___
Spa?	___	___	___	___	___	___	___
Other amenity?	___	___	___	___	___	___	___
Upgraded roof?	___	___	___	___	___	___	___
Upgraded windows?	___	___	___	___	___	___	___
Upgraded flooring?	___	___	___	___	___	___	___
Heating/cooling?	___	___	___	___	___	___	___
Electrical?	___	___	___	___	___	___	___
Plumbing?	___	___	___	___	___	___	___

Know which way the market is moving so that you can adjust your price accordingly. For example, if the market is moving up, you should be able to command more for your house than recent sales of comps (and sometimes prices for other "for sale" homes) reflect. Don't leave money on the table in a sale because you didn't forward price your home. (Similarly, if the trend is downward, your home may be worth somewhat less than recent sales reflect.)

Most local newspapers feature stories on the trends in real estate, especially in their Sunday editions. This has particularly been the case since the big price run-up of the past few years. However, other sources of price trends are available. Try the following:

- *www.realtrends.com*
- *www.realestatejournal.com*
- *www.hgtv.com*

Keep in mind that all trends are basically local. No matter what the national trend in housing might be, it only counts if it's happening in your area. Find out the local trends. Other sources include your local real estate board (through its agents) and the local chamber of commerce.

Local Job Market

People who are employed buy houses. People who are out of work don't. If the job market is healthy in your area, there should be many buyers ready, willing, and able to purchase. On the other hand, if local plants have shut down and many people are out of work, you're probably in a down market. Many out-of-work people may be trying to sell. And there could be few buyers.

This will affect how much you can ask, how quickly you can sell, and even if you should consider taking your home off the market to ride out the local depressed economy.

Information on jobs is readily available from the U.S. Department of Labor (*www.labor.org*). Also, local statistics on labor are available from many business groups as well as institutions of higher learning such as local colleges.

Interest Rates

Finally, you should keep in mind that real estate is highly sensitive to mortgage interest rates. Every time the interest rates go up 1 point, monthly payments rise, forcing hundreds of thousands of people nationwide out of the housing market (and that includes potential buyers for your property).

On the other hand, every time mortgage interest rates fall, hundreds of thousands of new buyers pour into the market because homes have just become more affordable.

KEY CONCEPT *The mortgage interest rate to watch is for the 30-year fixed-rate loan with no points. (Points are a percentage of the loan paid in cash up front that artificially lowers the interest rate.) Loans with points may have a lower interest rate, but they don't reflect the true market. Also, there are many loan alternatives for buyers, such as ARMs (adjustable rate mortgages) and Option Loans, which can temporarily produce a lower interest rate and lower payment, thus making it easier to buy a property. Even these, however, rise or fall as interest rates in general go up or down.*

If interest rates are rising, it will be harder to sell your home. You may have to take less to make your property more affordable . . . and it could take longer to sell. In a falling interest rate market, just the opposite is true.

The optimum interest rate is around 5 percent—that's an historical low. As of this writing, it's hovering between 6 and 7 percent. Anything over 7 percent is considered to be moderately high.

The national mortgage interest rate is widely reported each month in newspapers, on television, and on the radio. The mortgage interest rate for your state may vary slightly from the national, but usually not by much. Other sources for the current mortgage interest rate include:

- *www.bankratereporter.com*
- *www.mortgage.com*
- *www.eloan.com*

12 Finding the Optimum Agent

MARKETING YOUR HOME usually includes listing with an agent. (Unless, of course, you plan on selling it yourself; see Chapter 13.) Finding what I call the "optimum" agent is critical to a quick sale for a good price.

An "optimum" agent is one who will be able to do the most for you, quickly. It's important to understand that not every agent will fill this important function. While virtually all agents are more than willing to accept your listing, only a limited number have the tools, the energy, and the enthusiasm to move you forward to a quick sale.

In this chapter we're going to see how to find that one agent who has the qualities of an optimum agent—the one who will get the job done for you.

Where Do I Find Agents?

Be aware that there is no shortage of real estate agents. At last count, there were well over a million of them spread across the country. Were you to put a "For Sale" sign out in your yard on

Monday, chances are that by Tuesday half a dozen agents would be knocking on your door asking if they could list your property.

That's both good and bad. While finding an agent is easy, discerning the optimum agent from the herd can be more difficult.

My suggestion is that to begin, you look for agents who have been recommended. Ask friends, relatives, co-workers, anyone whose opinion you consider reliable. Have they recently sold (or bought) a home? Were they impressed by the agent they used? If so, can they give you his or her name and phone number? It's a good place to start.

If you can't get a recommendation, then I suggest you drive around your neighborhood and look for agents' "for sale" signs. These typically carry the listing agent's name on them. If one name consistently shows up, consider calling that person.

Agents "farm" neighborhoods. That means that they stake out a territory and try to become the one agent who knows the homes, the sellers, and the buyers in that area the best. Typically, this agent will have the most listings . . . and the most sales. If there is an optimum agent in your neighborhood, "for sale" signs and sometimes the word of neighbors can let you know who he or she is. (This agent will also occasionally come right up and knock on your door to introduce him- or herself.) Contacting this person is another good place to start.

Finally, I would contact a *local* real estate office, one that's near where your home is. But be careful. If you just walk in, chances are you'll be given to the next agent who's "up," the one designated to handle walk-in clients. This person is often new to the field, hence has time to deal with "drop-ins." What you want is a busy old-timer, someone who's experienced, has many contacts in the field, and knows how to sell. Ask to talk with the "top producer" in the office. Tell the receptionist that if he or she isn't available, you'll take his or her name and phone number and contact that person later.

Be aware that I have nothing against those new to the field—we all have to learn sometime. However, since I'm here making recommendations to you, the seller, my suggestion is that you go with experience and not with someone who's going to be learning on you.

Interview the Agent

Think of it as "hiring" an agent to work for you, even though you won't be paying them a salary. You want the optimum employee, even though the agent usually works on a commission basis. To find that person, you should interview them. Here are some of the questions you should ask:

- *Are you a* REALTOR®*?* The main trade organization in real estate is the NAR® (National Association of REALTORS). Any active agent should belong to it as well as the state organization and the local real estate board. If this agent doesn't, ask why. The REALTOR designation can only be used by members of the NAR. The NAR has a strict code of ethics that all members agree to follow, which benefits buyers and sellers.

- *Are you a broker or a salesperson?* Brokers are full-fledged agents; they can list, sell, rent, and collect commissions. They may also work under the auspices of another agent in a franchise company. (Many of the agents who work for companies such as Coldwell-Banker, Prudential, Sothebys, Century21, and others, are full brokers who have parked their license under the company name.) A salesperson usually must work under the supervision of a broker during an apprenticeship, typically two years. Only after that can he or she sit for a broker's license. Virtually all experienced agents I know are full brokers.

- *How long have you been in real estate?* We've already discussed this. The longer the agent has successfully been in the business, the more deals he or she presumably has handled with better contacts and more experience. If you want a quicker sale, get someone who knows how to do it.

- *How many hours a week do you spend selling real estate?* Some agents are part-time. They're retired and on pensions from other fields such as the military or teaching and only spend a few hours a week at real estate. There's nothing wrong with this. However, an active agent, one who spends 40 to 70 hours a week, is more likely to be on top of the market, have multiple clients waiting to buy, and know the best current approach to selling your property.

- *Are you a specialist?* Remember, you want someone local. Preferably, you want someone who farms the area in which your home is located. Ideally, the agent will even live nearby. This person often has the best shot at quickly coming up with a buyer for you.

- *How will you market my property?* Every operation needs a plan, and selling your house is no exception. You want to hear the agent rattle off a list of things he or she will do immediately to get your home in front of as many potential buyers as possible. (By the way, be wary of an agent who simply says, "We'll advertise it." Advertising is only one of many methods of attracting buyers.) Here's a list of potential ways of finding buyers for your home:
  - Spread the word to other agents through meetings, phone calls, bulletins, e-mails, and, of course, on the MLS.
  - Signs on your home and elsewhere.
  - Flyers mailed to known buyers.
  - Advertising in newspapers.
  - Listings on the Internet.
  - Open houses (more on this later).
  - Contacts with local transfer companies.
  - Contacts with local large employers.

- *Can you give me a list of references?* This is quite possibly the most important question to ask. An optimum agent should be able to hand you (or quickly prepare) a list of people whose homes he or she recently listed *and sold*. Tell the agent you'll make your listing decision soon. Then, after the agent has left, contact these people. Did they have a good experience? Most important, would they use the agent again?

The interviewing process need not last long. In half an hour you can often find out all the vitals. In a day or two you can interview three or four agents. If none fits the bill, keep looking. Remember, there's no shortage of agents. When one of them turns out to be the optimum agent, tell them you want to list.

What Kind of Listing Do You Want?

Typically you and the agent don't draw up a listing agreement together. Rather, the agent has the listing agreement all drawn up and merely wants you to sign. Be careful of what you sign. Listing agreements are intended to be legally binding documents—you could be held to their terms, and it could cost you money.

Some sellers will contact their lawyers before signing the agreement. Most sellers, however, simply check it over and if it meets with their approval, sign it.

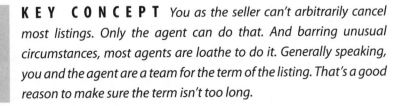

KEY CONCEPT *You as the seller can't arbitrarily cancel most listings. Only the agent can do that. And barring unusual circumstances, most agents are loathe to do it. Generally speaking, you and the agent are a team for the term of the listing. That's a good reason to make sure the term isn't too long.*

Here are some things that I suggest you check out in any listing agreement *before* you sign:

1. *Time limit:* All listing agreements should have a specified term. The most common term is 90 days. That should be enough for an optimum agent to find a buyer for your property. (Hopefully, they'll do it in a much shorter time period,

but no agent I know will accept a listing for less time, unless it's a one-day show of a FSBO; see Chapter 13.) Some agents will insist on 180 days or longer. I *never* give a listing for more than 90 days. If the house hasn't sold in 90 days and I'm satisfied the agent has worked hard, I can always renew for another 90 days. If I list for 180 days, I'm committed to that agent no matter how terrible a job he or she may do.

2. *Is it an exclusive right-to-sell listing?* An "exclusive right-to-sell" listing means that you'll pay the agent a commission no matter who sells the property, even if it's you! While intuitively you may not want this type of listing, it's actually the best for you. With this type of listing, the agent isn't worried you might undermine his or her efforts by selling the house out from under them directly to a buyer. This protection for the agent allows him or her to spend time, money, and energy on your property knowing that if he or she produces, he or she will get paid. Remember, keep your eye on the target—your goal is to sell the home, not avoid paying a commission to an agent.

3. *Is the commission rate what you want to pay?* There is no set commission rate in real estate. Rather, the commission is negotiated between seller and agent. As a seller, keep in mind that your goal is to sell your home, not cut the commission. If you can do both, fine. But beware of holding up the sale of your home because you're offering too low a commission. I always offer a full commission to any buyer's agent. (A buyer's agent is the one who brings in the buyer and represents him or her.) I'm willing to negotiate down the seller's (my) agent's commission. For example, if the listing agent wants a full commission of 6 percent, typically half goes to the office that finds the buyer and half to the listing office. To be sure agents work hard to find buyers, I don't try to negotiate down the 3 percent that goes to the buyer's agent's office. I may try to negotiate down the 3 percent that goes to the listing office.

4. *Are there any hidden fees?* Today, many listing offices throw in an additional "administrative" fee that goes not to the person with whom you're dealing directly, but to his or her office. Often this fee is a set amount, say, $350 or $500 or $700. This fee is over and above the listing commission, which is usually expressed as a percentage of the sales price. If you sign a listing with such a fee, you'll probably have to pay it when the deal closes. I consider this fee to be an unwarranted charge. I always "X" out such fees. Of course, that means the agent may not be willing to take my listing. But if that's the case, then I don't want that agent anyway.

5. *Do you understand the terms of the listing?* Remember, the listing is intended to be a legally binding document. Read it and be sure you understand it. If you don't understand something, ask for an explanation. If you're not satisfied with an explanation, have your lawyer reader it *before you sign*.

Once you've listed your property, you should work with your agent. Even though he or she is the one now responsible for bringing in a buyer, you still have to keep the ball rolling.

Keeping Your Property Ready to Show

Your end of it usually means keeping your property ready to show. While you may have staged it, it's still easy to get lazy. Keeping dishes in the dishwasher, pots and pans in the sink, the kitchen table not fully cleaned off, the beds not made, and so on—all these things and more have to be taken care of on a daily basis. The agent won't do them, so it's up to you.

Also, as noted in earlier chapters, you need to turn the lights on throughout the house before the agent shows the property, try to get some pleasant odors emanating from the kitchen, and leave some soothing music playing lightly on the stereo.

In short, all of the things you did to get your home in tip-top shape need to be maintained during the listing period and until the buyer shows up and you have a sale.

Tracking the Agent

The other thing you should do is to track your agent to make sure he or she is doing the job. Ideally, once we hire the agent, we should leave him or her alone to do his or her thing. However, too often I have seen sellers who wake up two or three months down the road only to discover that they made a mistake with the agent—the house hasn't sold and it's because the agent hasn't done the job. Better to find this out sooner than later when you might be able to do something about it.

Here's a list of things to keep track of with the agent. However, first a word about discretion. No one, especially not agents, likes to have someone breathing down his or her neck and looking over his or her shoulder. If you call your agent two or three times a day worrying over this and that, you'll be labeled a nuisance, and your agent may simply not pay any more attention to you.

On the other hand, a good agent will call you at least once a week to let you know what's being done to market your house and if any prospects have shown up. If the agent doesn't make that call, then you should call him or her. Simply say that you're curious to know how the marketing of your home is coming and ask if there has been any progress. That should earn you a full report. (Besides, your call lets the agent know you're interested and helps motivate him or her to keep working hard on selling your property.)

Here are some of the things you should ask about:

- *Have you spread the word?* Possibly the most effective thing that your agent can do is to spread the word of your home to other agents. Remember, between 85 and 90 percent of buyers buy homes through agents. The more individual agents are aware of your home and the benefits it offers, the better your chance for a quick sale. Ask your agent if he or she has:

- Prepared a "press release" on your home?
- Talked up your home at sales meetings?
- Called other agents (brokers and sales people) about it?
- Sent blanket e-mails to other offices?
- Otherwise contacted others in the field?

- *Have you contacted leads?* Agents often have clients waiting in the wings for homes to come on the market that fit their needs. You agent probably has many. Has he or she had a chance to talk with them about your home? What was the result?

- *Have you prepared a sign and flyer box?* Of course, you should know if your agent has or hasn't done this since it will be on your property. But if it hasn't been done, you should ask why. A sign on your property is considered crucial to finding buyers. After all, who knows if a neighbor might be interested in your home? Without a sign, how would they know it was for sale? Just as important, potential buyers cruising your neighborhood will see the sign and call the agent. The flyer box is attached to the sign and lets the casual person who's interested quickly learn the basics such as price, size, bedrooms and bathrooms, and so on by taking a flyer. It also helps them to remember the house they saw—your home.

- *Have you contacted other sources?* Yours may be the perfect home for an executive relocation. Almost all areas of the country have relocation services. If you've listed with a national real estate franchise, chances are they have their own relocation service. Has your agent made the necessary contacts? When will that be done?

- *Will your home be advertised?* Don't hold out excessive hope that your agent will find a buyer by advertising your home in the local newspaper. Most times buyers don't end up purchasing the home they called about from an ad. Yet, as part of an overall advertising plan, ads help. Ask when your home will appear in the realty ads. Ask to be sent a copy of the ad—it helps make sure that your home is included.

- *What about an open house?* As with newspaper advertising, open houses are overrated as a tool for finding a buyer for you. Indeed, the open house is actually a tool for the real estate agent to find potential buyers for other properties as well as to find more sellers who might list. In short, the open house tends to do the agent more good than you. But, it may do you some good too. I've purchased homes that I've first seen at an open house, as have others. Ask your agent when he or she will hold an open house. Try to get more than one.

- *What about a "caravan" and an "agent's open house"?* A caravan is when agents from your lister's office as well as other offices come by to see your house. An agent's open house is when the house is open just for agents, not buyers. (It's typically held on a weekday.) The entire purpose is to let other agents know about your property and get them excited about it, so they'll show it to their buyers. Your agent may ask you to put a spread out for the agents—small sandwiches, cookies, soft drinks (and sometimes wine). Yes, it might cost you a few bucks, but it's usually well worth the expense. If your agent doesn't ask you to pop for the spread, volunteer! It will impress your agent and may get him or her to make renewed efforts on your behalf.

- *Is it listed on the Internet?* Studies have repeatedly shown that more than half of all buyers first check the Internet for homes before contacting an agent. Indeed, buyers often contact agents about homes that they specifically saw on the Internet. That doesn't mean that because your home appears on the Internet it will automatically sell. What it does mean is that it's yet another means of marketing your home. Your REALTOR® should be able to get your home on *www.realtor.com,* the website of the NAR. It's one of the most widely hit sites on the Web and probably the most widely used real estate site. Most real estate offices also have their own websites where they can feature their listings. Make sure your agent gets your home up there on the Net where people can see it. And be sure the Internet listing includes photos. You'll want one of the outside of your home as well as several shots of the best rooms and features of your house. If you have a view lot, the view should also be shown. Remember, a picture is worth a thousand words, especially when attracting buyers.

13 Selling on Your Own for More Profit

SELLING ON YOUR own has a big advantage: it can save you the commission you'd otherwise pay to a real estate agent. For example, if your home sells for $350,000 and the commission is 6 percent, you can potentially save yourself $21,000. That's serious money, and I always suggest that if you have the time and inclination, you should certainly try selling FSBO (for sale by owner), at least for a while.

After all, just by planting a sign in your front yard with your phone number on it, you'll alert the world that your home is for sale. Who knows? Your neighbor across the street may be looking to buy a second home in the neighborhood as an investment or perhaps for a relative. Just with a sign, you'll alert that neighbor to your intentions, and you could get a quick sale.

Of course, that's a long shot. But trying to sell on your own for a few weeks usually won't hurt. And if you're a success, think of all the money you could save!

Note: Portions of this chapter first appeared in Robert Irwin, *The For Sale by Owner Kit* (Chicago: Dearborn Publishing, 2005). Check out that book for more details on how to sell your home by owner.

In point of fact, the vast majority of sellers use an agent. It's just simpler and easier . . . and often faster. Agents are set up to handle sales—after all, that's their business. You, on the other hand, have to quickly come up to speed on how to sell a home. Make no mistake; selling a home on your own doesn't mean doing anything less than an agent does. It just means *you* have to do the work the agent would otherwise do.

> **KEY CONCEPT** *FSBOs don't sell for more than homes that are listed. In today's market, price is critical. The biggest mistake you can make is to think, "Because I'm selling FSBO, I can ask more money for my house."*

To help you get started selling on your own, here are some items that you'll need to sell FSBO. It's not particularly hard, but it can be tricky.

Don't Overprice

You probably won't make this critical error. Just remember, buyers don't care if it's listed, FSBO, or auctioned. They are interested in only paying a competitive price. Give the buyers the right price and they'll buy as well from you as from an agent.

To you, selling FSBO may be significant. It may mean that you're putting in lots of time and effort. It's only natural, therefore, that as a FSBO seller you want to recoup the time, money, and effort from the buyer. It's not unreasonable to feel that you are entitled to ask more for your house.

The truth, unfortunately, is that entitled or not, you can get only what the house is worth on the market. You can ask anything that you want, but you'll only get what buyers are willing to pay.

Price it too high, and your house will sit there, not selling, while other homes, priced only a few thousand less, may be sold in days.

Make Arrangements for Handling the Documents

How are you going to draw up the sales agreement? What about the disclosures and the other documentation needed?

If you're familiar with real estate and have done many transactions, then this won't seem like such a barrier. But if this is all fairly new to you, then you may be justifiably concerned about getting it right. Remember, most of these are intended to be legally binding documents. Screw them up and you could be in hot water.

Fortunately, there are options available to you these days. Now is the time to decide which you want to use. Discount brokers and fee-for-service agents are available in many areas. Oftentimes, they will handle all the paperwork for you for a set fee.

Consider hiring a real estate attorney, if there's one available in your area. In some areas, particularly the East Coast, real estate attorneys will handle all the paperwork for a set fee, often under $1,500. It's a cost-effective way of getting it done right.

It's important that you consider these alternatives and make a decision on how you're going to handle the documents before you list with yourself. It's too late to start thinking about that when you have a buyer in hand. You might lose that buyer if you appear unsure of yourself at a critical moment.

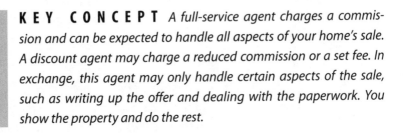

KEY CONCEPT *A full-service agent charges a commission and can be expected to handle all aspects of your home's sale. A discount agent may charge a reduced commission or a set fee. In exchange, this agent may only handle certain aspects of the sale, such as writing up the offer and dealing with the paperwork. You show the property and do the rest.*

Market Your Home on the Internet

List your house on several of the many online FSBO services. Many of these will provide you with a sign and help with the paperwork.

It's a fact that most buyers first check out the Internet before physically looking for a home. Many visit by owner sites. Be sure that they see your home there.

Many of these sites also give you the opportunity to put up images of your home. You can shoot these with a small digital camera and upload them on a home computer—it's easy. Be sure to do it. Remember how much a picture is worth.

Sites to consider include:

- *www.owners.com*
- *www.fsbo.com*
- *www.forsalebyowner.com*

Market Your Home Locally

Get your own "For Sale" sign and display it prominently in your front yard. As noted, some Internet sites offer these signs. Also, virtually all discount brokers offer them as well. If you do decide to make your own, be sure it looks professional. An amateurish sign could scare prospective buyers away from dealing directly with you.

Prepare leaflets describing your property, including a picture, and distribute them widely. Build an information box and attach it to your sign. Put flyers up on bulletin boards in public buildings, the housing offices of corporations, and even on display panels in supermarkets. And advertise.

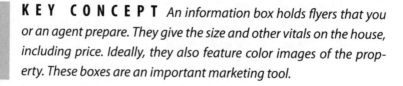

KEY CONCEPT *An information box holds flyers that you or an agent prepare. They give the size and other vitals on the house, including price. Ideally, they also feature color images of the property. These boxes are an important marketing tool.*

Your ad doesn't have to be big (often only three or four lines will do), but it should run regularly, and you should change it often (so that buyers don't recognize it as the same property and ignore it).

Also, find out whether inexpensive advertising is available on local radio and cable TV stations. (There often is.) Try a 30-second commercial there. The right slant can bring you amazing results.

Talk up your property to all of your acquaintances whether or not they're interested in buying. Someone may know a friend of a friend who's interested, and that person might ultimately become your buyer.

Finally, be friendly with real estate agents when they come by (and they will!). Tell them that right now you're trying to sell on your own as a FSBO. But if you don't sell within a reasonable amount of time, you'll consider working through them. Tell them that at that point, you'll pay a buyer's-agent commission if they find a buyer. (Remember from Chapter 12 that it's half a full commission.)

Talk to agents and be friendly. Remember, they are in the business of finding buyers. It would be foolish to ignore them, particularly when you can get them to work for you.

Consider Having Your Home Listed on the MLS

Today, many discount brokers will list your home on the MLS (Multiple Listing Service) for a set fee, often between $500 and $1,000. This is the service that brokers use to cooperate on listings.

If you're willing to pay half a commission (the buyer's broker's part), why not list on the MLS? After all, that's the same amount that buyers' agents get if they sell a home that's fully listed by an agent. So, you'll get the benefit of the MLS exposure, if not the full efforts of a listing agent.

Remember, agents use the MLS to work together. There might be as many as a thousand or more agents in your area. If a home is listed on the MLS, it's available to all of them. Currently 85 to 90 percent of home buyers first contact an agent, so by putting your home on the MLS you buy into this network.

Offer to Finance the Sale

This applies whether you're selling FSBO or listing with an agent. Housing prices today are high. That means that at any given time, the number of people who can qualify for a given house is limited. In short, houses are getting less affordable. (A recent index in California, for example, indicated that in some areas of that state less than 25 percent of buyers could afford the median-priced home!)

This translates into two very powerful problems:

1. Fewer people have the cash for the down payment necessary for a purchase.
2. Even fewer have the income and excellent credit needed to qualify for a big low-down- or nothing-down mortgage.

Ideally you'll probably want the buyer to come in for all cash to you (through financing). However, that may not always be possible. And the easier you can make the purchase for the buyer, the better the chances are that your house will sell before your neighbor's house does.

There is a way you can help the buyer. You can carry back a portion of the sales price in the form of a second (or third) mortgage. Or, you can fold most of the buyer's closing costs into a similar mortgage.

If the buyer doesn't have a lot of cash and can't get a low-down/nothing-down mortgage, you can help by carrying back 10 percent as a second mortgage. The buyer might put down 10 percent, you'd carry back 10 percent, and the buyer might be able to get an easier qualifying 80 percent mortgage. Or, if the lender is willing, agree to a higher sales price with the difference (between the old sales price and the new) folded into the buyer's new, bigger mortgage to cover most of the closing costs.

The point is that when you make it easier for buyers to purchase, you make it easier on yourself to sell. It's like a pyramid. Those with less money and less income are at the wider bottom.

Those with more money and more income are at the pointed top. The more you can appeal to those at the bottom of the pyramid, the bigger the base of potential buyers you can attract.

Create a Plan for Showing Your Home

The minute you decide to sell FSBO, you're committing to doing the work of showing your home yourself. Unfortunately, this means giving up some of your free time. It means that you must be willing to sit at home waiting for buyers to show up. If a buyer calls you at eight in the morning on Sunday while you're still sleeping, you'll agree to show the property at nine, even though it means jumping out of bed and working frantically to get the place ready.

Being available for buyers means keeping at least one phone line clear. If you're going to be gone, it means using call forwarding, an answering machine, a cell phone, or a family member to catch incoming calls. It means that you're ready to show the house every day of the week and that it's clean all of those days.

Don't bother to sell FSBO unless you're willing to do all of the tasks described. If you're half-hearted about it, if you decide to take a two-week vacation three days after putting the sign in the front yard, if you tell a buyer who calls that you've got to go to your mother's house for lunch and can't show the property, then don't bother to sell FSBO. Bite the bullet and list.

When you list with yourself, you must make the commitments necessary to sell your home successfully. One of the biggest commitments is time. If you can't spend the time, list with an agent who can. A FSBO seller must show the house. That's just the way it is.

Until you get the appropriate signatures on the dotted line, you're a slave to buyers. To think anything else is to do yourself a disservice. To attempt to sell FSBO without making yourself and the property always available is simply to be playing at it.

If you truly want to sell FSBO, you'll make the time. If you find that you simply can't make the necessary time, then I strongly suggest you reconsider listing with a full-service agent.

Work on Your Salesmanship

Some people feel that a good salesperson can sell ice cubes to Eskimos and sunlamps to Hawaiians. If you're this type of salesperson, you can sell your house on your own by next week without my or anyone else's help.

On the other hand, if you're a normal human being, you may get along fairly well with people, but you don't have any super talents when it comes to selling. Rest assured, you don't need any.

I have found that when selling real estate, or anything else for that matter, the key is to establish a relationship of trust with the person to whom you're selling. Sell yourself first. Beyond that, the product should sell itself, assuming it doesn't have a problem.

If you establish a working relationship with the buyer and have a good house that the buyer wants, you merely have to nod in the right places, point out the obvious, reassure the faint of heart, and sign on the dotted line. If you have a bad house or the buyer doesn't want it, you're not going to sell it to that prospect now or later, so don't worry about it.

How do you establish trust? Do what comes natural—be honest.

Always Have a Backup Plan

Selling your home is like launching a military campaign . . . and you're the general. Any good general is not only going to have a plan "A," which he or she hopes will lead to immediate success, but also a plan "B" on which to fall back on if "A" doesn't work out.

For example, you've decided that you're willing to give a 1 percent commission to a discount broker who will handle all of the paperwork for you. However, for 1 percent the broker may not list the home on the MLS (Multiple Listing Service). Indeed, to get it listed the discount broker may recommend you pay not only its 1 percent, but an additional 3 percent to a buyer's broker for a total of 4 percent to you—plus $500 or so for the actual listing.

While this may seem unreasonably high right now, it might not seem so several months down the road *if* your home hasn't sold. So your backup plan may look like this. List now for 1 percent and give it two full weeks, during which time you'll advertise and otherwise promote your home. Then, and only then, if the home doesn't sell, call the discount broker and list it on the MLS.

Finally, if all else fails, consider listing it with a full-service broker. (You can't normally list it twice—simultaneously with a discount broker and with a full-service broker—so first make up your mind which way you're going to jump.)

I always suggest that sellers try to sell FSBO for a few weeks. As noted at the beginning of this chapter, you never know: a neighbor might be ready to buy your home. Then, if things don't work out, don't waste a lot of time. List with a professional and get that quick sale.

Get It on Paper

When you've got your buyer ready to sign on the dotted line, be sure you have a dotted line for him or her to sign on. You need to have a purchase agreement ready to go (see the section on documentation). If you're working with a fee-for-service or discount broker, they should be able to handle the sales agreement for you. Otherwise, have your lawyer prepare it for you.

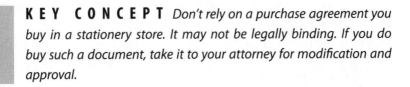

K E Y   C O N C E P T *Don't rely on a purchase agreement you buy in a stationery store. It may not be legally binding. If you do buy such a document, take it to your attorney for modification and approval.*

Keep in mind that according to the statute of frauds adopted in all states, an agreement to purchase real estate must be in writing. Otherwise it won't be enforceable.

The sales agreement is the most important document of the sale because it governs all the others. Once you have a completely filled out and signed sales agreement, you'll need to open escrow (unless an agent is also handling this for you).

There are many escrow companies, and you should shop around for the one that offers you the lowest prices. You may need to pay for all or some escrow services and title insurance for the buyer. Usually an escrow runs for 30 to 45 days. How long is determined by need and what's written into the sales agreement. (Who pays what for escrow is determined by local custom; the escrow company can clue you into the usual arrangements in your area; see also Chapter 15 for details on handling the closing.)

Chances are your buyers will want a home inspection, and you'll need to provide them with disclosures. Check with any agent who is assisting you for the exact forms required for your state and locale. The important thing here is that you comply with deadlines and disclose all defects. You don't want a buyer coming back years later to hound you over a problem that turned up that you failed to disclose.

Also, should there be a defects in your title, you'll need to clear them up. A defect is something such as a lien you forgot to pay off years ago. Perhaps you were sued by a credit company, and they filed against the property. Or perhaps there was a court settlement that was paid off, but the records never reflected it. It's up to you to solve the problem. (Check with an attorney on these.)

If all goes well, there will come a day when you are notified that escrow is ready to close. For you, as the seller, there's not much more to do than to approve the final escrow instructions (which say who gets paid for what) and sign off on the deed to be given to the buyer.

Finally, when the buyer and the lender deposit funds, the escrow will close and you'll get a call saying your check is ready to be picked up. Chances are it will be one of the best days of your life!

Be Prepared

You don't have to be a Boy Scout to sell your home on your own. If you're willing to do the work and spend the time and energy, you can do it. Many, many other sellers already have.

The trouble is, it may not sell on the first day or the first week, or even the first month. Time may become something you'll learn to hate. You'll stay home on weekends waiting for someone to call or knock on your door. Or, suddenly, three or four people will call and then come rushing by. Or you'll spend so much time cleaning and polishing, painting and trimming that you'll be sick of it. You'll begin to tell yourself you need a vacation from house selling!

In the short term, you may come to hate your house and the process of selling it.

Which, of course, is why most people list.

I'm not trying to discourage you from selling FSBO. Actually, I encourage you to give it a try. Just be realistic. Rome wasn't built in a day, and your home may not sell FSBO in one, either.

Steps to Selling Your Home by Owner

1. Fix it.
2. Stage it.
3. Make the decision to go FSBO.
4. Price it right (not more than for a listed home).
5. Make arrangements for a pro to handle the documents.
6. Prepare a marketing campaign.
7. Show your home.
8. Offer financing.
9. Find a buyer.
10. Get it down on paper.
11. Open escrow.
12. Close the deal.

14 Negotiating to Get Your Price

AFTER ALL THE work, time, and money spent fixing, staging, and currying buyers, you get an offer!

It's time for champagne toasts!

No, not really. An offer isn't a sale. It's just what it says it is—an offer to purchase for a certain price at certain terms by a buyer.

Most offers are for less than the asking price. (In times of hot markets, sometimes offers can actually be for more than the asking price; we'll discuss this shortly.)

Now you have to make a decision. Do you accept whatever offer the buyer has made? Or do you reject it outright? Or do you reject it and then counter with something of your own?

KEY CONCEPT *You can't both accept and counter. Any changing of the price or terms of the buyer's offer rejects it. Be wary of agents who sometimes say confusing things such as, "Let's accept what the buyer's offering, only ask for more money." Once you ask for more money (or change the terms), the offer's rejected.*

As I said, chances are that in most markets, the offer you get will be for less than your asking price. If that happens, what do you do?

When the Buyer Low-Balls You

The buyer's offer may only be a few hundred dollars less than you're asking. In that case, if you're happy with the price, simply accept it.

On the other hand, many times you'll get a low-ball offer. This can be for significantly less than you're asking. For example, your asking price may be $350,000 and the buyer comes in at $275,000. That's more than a 20 percent cut in your asking price—quite a low-ball, and not something that most sellers would be happy about.

At this point, you have to ask yourself, "Why is the buyer offering so much less?"

Presumably you've done your homework and checked out the comparables, adjusted for market conditions and other factors, and priced your home right (see Chapter 11.) Now you remember my earlier words and ask, "Dear author, you said that buyers today were savvy. Why doesn't this buyer see that I've priced my home correctly and offer accordingly?"

Don't panic. There are three basic reasons for a lowball offer:

1. The buyer is an investor who wants to "steal" your home.
2. The buyer simply can't afford the price you're asking and is desperate to get into your home and neighborhood.
3. The buyer legitimately wants to buy and is just "feeling you out" to see how desperate to sell you might be.

Let's consider each reason separately:

The Investor Buyer

This person is looking to make money on the purchase. If he or she can buy your home for below market, it can be quickly flipped and sold for a profit: buy the home for $275,000 (in our example), and then turn around and resell it for full price—$350,000. Instead of you making $75,000, the buyer makes it.

Do you want to give an investor most of your equity? Probably not. Remember, there's nothing illegal about what this buyer is doing. He or she is just offering you a way out, hoping you're desperate enough to take it. Hopefully, you're not that desperate.

The Desperate Buyer

This person probably loves your home and your neighborhood. But he or she simply doesn't have the cash, credit, and/or income to buy it at market price. So, the offer is made on a hope and a prayer. Maybe, just maybe, you'll consider selling for a ridiculously low price.

My heart goes out to this buyer. In these times of very high home prices, increasingly there are buyers just like this who want to get in, but simply can't afford to.

As I said, my heart goes out to them . . . but not my wallet. If you want to turn the sale of your home into a charity, by all means accept. Otherwise, move on.

The Testing Buyer

This is a savvy buyer who knows what your home is worth (presumably, if you've done your homework, what you're asking for it). But he or she doesn't want to leave any money on the table. Why pay more, if they can pay less?

So this offer is to test the waters. If you're a desperate (called "highly motivated") seller, you just might accept, or at least counter at a much lower price than you're asking. The buyer loses relatively little by making such a trial offer (although if you simply walk away from it, it makes coming back with a higher offer more difficult) and can gain a great deal if you accept.

What You Should Do

What you do is up to you. Ask your agent and a trusted financial adviser. Everyone's situation is different.

What I usually do is to counter a first low-ball offer. (Remember, by countering I've rejected the offer.) If I've done my homework and am sure my original asking price is right, I might, for example, drop my price by $500. In our example of an asking price of $350,000 where the buyer offers $275,000, I might counter at $349,500.

But, you may be thinking to yourself, the counter is as ridiculous as the original offer! The buyer offers $75,000 less than I'm asking. The counter is for $74,500 more than the offer. No way is there a compromise here.

True. My counter is not an attempt to compromise. It's designed to accomplish two things:

1. I let the buyer know that I'm not desperate to sell. Rather, I think my asking price is fair and I'm pretty sure I'll get it.

2. I give the buyer an honorable way to come back and pay my price. I don't laugh at the buyer's offer (which might be how he or she would interpret a total rejection of it). Rather, I'm saying, "OK, you've given a shot and tried low-balling. Now, let's see if you're really a serious buyer."

The Buyer's Response to My Counter

At this point, the buyer has a choice. As a seller, I've made it clear that I won't be low-balled. What is the buyer to do?

An investor buyer probably will simply move on, and you'll never hear from him or her again. This type of buyer often makes dozens, sometimes hundreds, of low-ball offers on all kinds of properties, hoping that just by sheer chance one of them will connect with a highly motivated seller. You're not that seller; you're not going to sell for a low-ball price, so it's on to the next property.

Sometimes this buyer will come back with his or her own counter for roughly the same amount as the original lowball offer. It's asking, "Are you sure?" If you're sure, you may want to simply reject this second low-ball counter out of hand—I would.

The desperate buyer, on the other hand, would love to pay your price—but can't. I've seen such buyers repeat their original offer including a poignant letter explaining why they need your home and would love and cherish it, if only you would consider their plight and come down in price. Again, if you're charitable by nature and want to make them your project, accept. It's your money. I would simply reject the offer.

Finally, the real buyer who's testing will now have to either fish or cut bait. I would expect this buyer to now make a more reasonable counteroffer, or even to accept your counter.

What, you may be saying? The buyer would come up nearly $75,000?!

Yep. Happens all the time. Remember, with this buyer, the first offer was a test. Now, it's time for the real offer. It might be within a few thousand of your asking price, in which case you'll want to see whether you're willing to risk losing a sale for such a small amount of money (given the overall price). Or, if the buyer is afraid of losing out on your home, the offer might be for full price. Either way, you're close to selling your home.

When the Offer Is for the Asking Price or More

This happens in a hot market and happened frequently a few years back. You may get multiple offers at or above your asking price. Most sellers are thrilled. Don't be. It means you didn't price your home at market but instead priced it too low.

Now you have to decide which offer to accept. Or, if you're clever and savvy, you can start a bidding war between the buyers. Your agent (or attorney) can assist you with writing counters to each of the multiple offers, which allow the buyers to bid against each other to get you the highest price.

W A R N I N G *Be wary of agents who suggest you list below market price in order to encourage a bidding war. Sometimes it works. But, if it doesn't, you could end up being forced to either accept a low-ball offer or pay a commission not to sell! (The agent usually has earned a commission when he or she brings in a buyer ready, willing, and able to purchase at your asking price and terms; if you ask too low, you could owe a commission even if you don't sell!)*

The Risk of Countering

It's important to understand the consequences when you counter a buyer's offer. One of the most important, which we've already mentioned, is that you reject that offer. It's gone, off the table. The buyer can simply ignore your counter (see above) and walk away. Now, you have no offer.

Of course, if you feel you've made a mistake by rejecting and countering, you can try to resurrect that buyer's original offer. You can direct your agent to tell the buyer that you've changed your mind. You'd love to accept it exactly as written. Unfortunately, by then the buyer may already be off and looking at other houses, and may even have found and made an offer on another house.

In short, when you counter a buyer's offer, you stand a chance of losing out on that buyer entirely. The only way to ensure that you've got that buyer is to accept the offer in its entirety—price and all its terms. It's something to consider.

On the other hand, when you make a counteroffer, you've committed yourself to what you're offering. If it's less than the asking price or at lesser terms than you originally wanted, and the buyer accepts your counter exactly as offered, then you're committed to it.

Don't counter under the assumption that the buyer will reject or counter your offer. The buyer may accept it outright . . . and you've got a deal. When you counter, make sure it's a deal you really want.

Of course, the buyer is under the same constraints with your counter. If you make a counteroffer, and the buyer rejects it and counters back, you're under no obligation to accept the buyer's new counteroffer. You're back to square one. You can accept it as is. Or reject and counter again.

Thus, the negotiations can go on for hours and sometimes days in this fashion until a deal is finally hammered out or both parties decide that no deal is possible.

When to Do It

An important part of this negotiation process is time. In fact, most purchase agreements have a clause in them that says, "time is of the essence" for the contract. That means that if a deadline passes or is ignored, it has consequences.

For example, most purchase agreements will give you a certain amount of time to consider the offer and to accept or reject it. It could be three days, or 12 hours, or whatever. The buyer is offering to hold the offer open during that time period. If you accept the offer in its entirety during that time period, presumably you've got a deal. If you fail to act during that time period and you pass the deadline, the offer is off the table.

> **W A R N I N G** *Just because a buyer puts a deadline on an offer doesn't mean he or she is totally committed to it. Technically, the buyer can withdraw the offer at any time prior to your signing it in its entirety and that fact being communicated back to the buyer. For example, the buyer gives you a day to sign. You're mulling it over, thinking, yes, you'll probably accept. In the meantime, the buyer finds another house she likes better and tells his or her agent to withdraw the offer to you, even though the deadline hasn't passed. You haven't signed, the offer is withdrawn ... you lose. (The same applies to any counters you make.) That's a good reason to make up your mind and act in a timely fashion.*

Beginning real estate agents often go out of their way to insist that buyers put in a long time for acceptance. For example, they may give you a week to accept. If you're a savvy seller, you may say thanks, and notwithstanding the fact that the offer could be withdrawn at any time, take the full week. You hope that during that week a better offer may come in. If one doesn't, you'll accept this one.

A more savvy agent will insist the buyer only give you the shortest of times, say until 12 midnight of the day the offer is made. That forces you to accept it or take a chance on losing out on a sale. It doesn't give you time to hang on to it waiting for something better to come along.

Putting the pressure on you to sign is an old-fashioned way of squeezing you. It forces you to make a decision when you'd probably rather sleep on it . . . or at least think it over for a few days.

On the other hand, sometimes the best results come when you're under pressure. As they say, nothing focuses the mind like pressure. The buyers may be doing you a favor by forcing you to decide. You'll reassess your situation, talk it over with others such as spouse and financial advisers, and make your move. Oftentimes, moves made in such a way are better than those that are dragged out over time.

Items to Check in the Offer

Thus far, we've been discussing the offer as if it were fully acceptable, except for price. But what about terms? Sometimes the price can be okay, but the terms are unacceptable.

It's impossible to anticipate the myriad terms a buyer might offer. However, here are some of the more common and what they might mean to you.

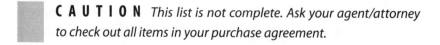

CAUTION *This list is not complete. Ask your agent/attorney to check out all items in your purchase agreement.*

The Deposit

It's normal for the buyer to put up a deposit as a show of earnestness. Years ago, the deposit was critical to making the deal. Today, with so many contingencies, it's less so.

Nonetheless, a deposit is usually in order. Typically, it's $5,000 or more and is presumably at risk if the buyer backs out without a justifiable reason.

Don't count on getting that deposit any time soon. Today, most transactions, sometimes up to the very last minute, have so many escape clauses built into them that buyers frequently can walk away . . . with their deposit. Check with your agent/attorney if you're not sure about your buyer's deposit.

Financing

Most offers that aren't for cash will include a financing contingency. It will say something to the effect that if the buyer can't get needed financing (as described in the offer), the deposit is to be returned and the deal is off.

 C A U T I O N *You may want to add your own contingency that if the buyer has trouble securing financing, you can keep your house on the market to secure backup offers.*

There's nothing wrong with this; after all, how can the buyer be expected to make the purchase without a needed loan? What could be wrong comes about if the buyer isn't able to obtain financing. You could agree to the deal only to find a month or so down the road that the buyer never could qualify for a mortgage and you've wasted your time. One way to avoid this problem is to insist that the buyer show you a pre-approval letter *from a lender* stating the buyer is qualified to get the needed loan and the lender is ready to fund as soon as the property qualifies through an appraisal. Another way is to insist that the buyer provide a lender willing to fund within two weeks.

Appraisal

While it often isn't specifically spelled out, the financing on the property hinges on your property appraising for a high enough amount so that the buyer can get a needed loan. For example, you're selling for $200,000 and the buyer needs a 95 percent mortgage or $190,000.

However, the lender's appraiser says your property is only worth $195,000 and a 95 percent loan only comes to $185,250. The buyer can't get the needed financing. Essentially you're short almost $5,000 to make the deal.

What do you do? Here are some options:

- Get a reappraisal from the same lender (which probably won't change).
- Get a new lender and a new appraiser.
- Reduce your price the $5,000 (something you don't want to do).
- Have the buyer put up an extra $5,000 in cash (something he or she probably can't or doesn't want to do).
- Lend the buyer the difference in the form of a second mortgage.
- Compromise and do a little of this and a little of that.

Appraisals can be tricky, and often low appraisals can destroy a deal. You should be aware of this possibility when you sign a purchase agreement and be ready to deal with it if it arises.

Escrow Time

Escrow (during which time the title to the property is checked, the buyer secures financing, and other necessary matters are dealt with) typically runs 30 to 45 days. Some buyers (or sellers), however, will want more or less.

Be sure the time period for escrow is to your liking and that you've agreed to it. Remember, once you sign, you're committed to what the document says.

Occupancy

When does the buyer get to move in?

Normally it's when escrow closes. But, sometimes the buyers will specify they want to move in before the close of escrow. If you sign, then that's the deal. Remember, though, a buyer who moves in before escrow closes becomes a tenant. If everything goes according to plan and escrow closes on schedule, there's little problem. (But, you may want to insist on rent during that period.) But, if escrow doesn't close in a timely manner, you've got a tenant you might not be able to easily remove from your house. If escrow never closes, you might have to go through eviction proceedings to get that tenant out!

Be careful about letting a buyer in before escrow closes. If you do, have the buyer sign a solid rental agreement and put up a security/cleaning deposit in cash (in addition to the purchase deposit). And be aware of the potential consequences. (You might also want to check out my book *The Landlord's Trouble Shooter* [Chicago: Dearborn Publishing, 2004.])

Personal Property

Sometimes the buyer will include a list of your personal property he or she wants included in the sale. It can include such things as furniture, a refrigerator, lawn chairs, and so on. If you agree, they must go with the sale.

Of course, you can refuse and insist the buyer pay for these outside of the purchase agreement. That, of course, involves another whole set of negotiations.

Sometimes to avoid such problems, sellers will include a list of personal property included and not included in the sale. A better approach, however, is to remove any personal property you don't want included in the deal before you put the home up for sale. What buyers don't see, they won't covet.

Other Conditions

The buyers might include all kinds of other conditions in the purchase. For example, the purchase might be contingent on them selling stock at a certain price to get the money for the down payment. Or the purchase might be subject to their getting a new job in your area. Or . . . ?

There's no end to the possibilities.

My suggestion is that you consider each carefully. Ask yourself, Is it realistic? What is the risk to you? And then decide whether to go along with it.

A savvy seller may decide to reject a full-price offer *if* the terms aren't acceptable.

Get Escrow Opened and Instructions Signed

Finally, once you do get a deal with everyone signed off, be sure you or your agent (or the buyer's agent) quickly opens escrow. This moves the deal forward and helps ensure that it's a "done deal."

The first thing an escrow officer will do is read the purchase agreement and draw up instructions to escrow. These instructions detail what must be done to complete the transaction. You'll be given a set as will the buyers.

Read them carefully!

Be sure the instructions to escrow accurately reflect the purchase agreement you signed. I've found that too often escrow officers misinterpret details, and the instructions aren't what you actually agreed to. If they're wrong, point it out and have them redrawn accurately. (If you let them go, you could end up with a different deal!)

You and the buyers will be asked to sign the escrow instructions. These are again intended to be legally binding documents and help cement the transaction.

15 Closing the Deal

CONGRATULATIONS!

You've fixed up your home.

You've staged it.

And you've sold it.

You've opened escrow and now you're waiting to get your check and move!

Not quite so fast. There are a few more things that you need to do before you can "get out of Dodge." You have to make sure that escrow closes.

The concept of having a deal within a deal tends to be foreign to those unfamiliar with real estate. But, that's what this is really all about.

Think of the purchase agreement and the escrow instructions you signed as the preliminaries. Now you're at the main event. Here the buyer has to perform (and so do you) for the deal to close.

Your agent should track escrow and take care of any problems that arise. But, if you're selling FSBO, or just to follow-up on your agent, you also should track what's to be done.

Here's a list of items that usually need to be accomplished for escrow to close and your house to actually sell:.

Escrow Tracking

Buyer	Seller
Put up cash for down payment	Clear title
Put up cash for closing	Secure termite report
Secure financing	Repair termite damage
Sign off on disclosures	Repair fungus damage
Sign off on inspections	Get termite clearance
Sign off on contingencies	Secure other reports
Get funded	Get clearances
Sign loan documents	Sign deed
Anything else needed	Anything else needed

What Escrow Will and Won't Do

Escrow's job is to gather all the money and needed paperwork and, when everything is perfect, close. That means record the loan for the lender, record the deed for the buyer, and give you your money.

Along the way, escrow will prepare many documents. But, it won't take action. For example, it will tell you (through a title search) if there are any hidden liens on your property. These can occur from years past when you failed to pay off a debt and the lender, through a quiet court action, got a judgment against you and recorded it on your property. Now, you'll have to pay it off (or get it removed) to deliver clear title and be able to sell.

Or perhaps there's an easement to a utility company that you didn't even know about that's clogging the title. You may need to hire a lawyer to get is cleared.

Or what about getting a termite/fungus inspection? And then getting the work done and a clearance issued?

Escrow may let you know it needs to be done. But it won't normally lift a finger to do it. Rather, you (or your agent) will have to do all the heavy lifting.

That means, you'll need to clear liens; handle easements; get the termite report, work, and clearance; and do everything else necessary to be able to give clear title to the buyer and sell your home.

Your agent should be on top of all of it. But, it won't hurt to call your agent and/or escrow once a week (at the minimum) to see how things are progressing. If your agent should fall down on the job, to close the deal you'll need to take up the slack. From escrow find out what's needed, prod your agent, or do it yourself.

And that's just your end of the deal!

The Buyer's Responsibilities

While you're off doing your things, the buyers and their agent have a whole separate list of things to do. And here's where it gets tricky.

As a seller, not only should you be keeping tabs on your agent and escrow to see your end of the deal is coming together, you should also keep tabs on the buyer's end of the deal as well! After all, what good does it do you to clear title if the buyer ultimately can't qualify and get a mortgage? The deal's dead anyway.

Thus, your agent (or you if your agent falls down on the job) needs to be contacting escrow and the buyer's agent (or the buyer directly if there's no agent involved) to see how things are coming. Has the buyer approved the inspection report? No? Why not? What doesn't the buyer like? What needs to be done to correct the situation? In many deals, the buyers have several weeks to approve the inspection report. They don't approve it? The deal could be off. Wouldn't you like to know that as soon as possible so you can get your home back on the market?

What about the disclosures? Have the buyers approved them? Did they sign off? In many states the buyers have a statutory period of time to look over the disclosures and if they don't approve, the deal's off. (In California, it's three days from the time they physically receive them.) Did the buyers get your disclosures? (You did fill them out, didn't you?!) If the buyers don't get the disclosure until escrow is ready to close, they may have an easy way to "walk" without penalty—just disapprove them. Hence, you want those disclosures delivered to the buyer and their approval secured ASAP.

And most important, there's the financing. Remember, no buyer financing, in most cases, no deal.

Be sure your agent, or you, track how the buyer's financing is coming along. If after a few weeks it becomes apparent they're having trouble, you may want to put your home back on the market (if allowed by the purchase agreement, a contingency you may want included before you sign; see the chapter 14).

I generally call my agent and the escrow company once a week to see if there are any problems developing with the buyer's financing. If I sniff trouble, I also call the buyer's agent, and if necessary, the buyers directly. (You can try calling the buyer's lender, but most times, because of privacy issues, you won't get anywhere.) If the deal is going to fall apart because of financing issues, you want to know ASAP and get the house back on the market.

Hopefully, everything will go as planned. Escrow will close on time, and you'll get your money.

Final Walkthrough

But, before escrow finally closes, there's the legendary "final walkthrough."

In today's real estate market, buyers usually include a contingency in the purchase agreement that allows them to come back one last time to inspect your home, just before the close of escrow. The purported purpose is to make sure that the property is as it was when you sold it to them. (After all, you could have had a few orgies and messed up the place. Or you could have removed items that were to have stayed. Or . . . ? The buyers, understandably, want to see that things haven't changed during the month or so escrow takes.)

It's not unreasonable. And, it's a good reason for you as a seller to maintain your property in tip-top shape during the escrow period. (Another good reason is that if the deal falls through and escrow doesn't close, you want to be able to quickly put it back on the market.)

Usually you will have already moved out when the buyers come through. Moving out often reveals scratches on walls, tears on carpets, and so on that were hidden by the furniture. (You probably didn't know about them yourself.) You may need to come back and fix these. Or pay the buyer a few bucks as compensation.

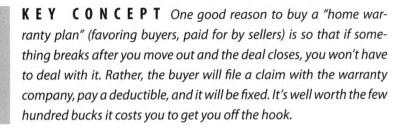

K E Y   C O N C E P T *One good reason to buy a "home warranty plan" (favoring buyers, paid for by sellers) is so that if something breaks after you move out and the deal closes, you won't have to deal with it. Rather, the buyer will file a claim with the warranty company, pay a deductible, and it will be fixed. It's well worth the few hundred bucks it costs you to get you off the hook.*

Walkthrough Problems

Usually the only problems that occur are when the buyers discover something serious during the walkthrough. Of course, if your home is properly fixed up and staged, they shouldn't find anything serious. But, if they do, you'll have to deal with it.

Serious trouble can occur when what the buyers find isn't real—rather, they just want to back out of the deal at the last minute and are using the final walkthrough as an excuse. That can be difficult.

For example, the buyers say there are cracks in the cement patio. They weren't there before. Now they don't want the house.

You argue the cracks have been there for 20 years. The buyers say, nope. They're new. (Of course, if you had mentioned the cracks in your disclosures, which the buyers had approved by signing, it shouldn't be much of a problem. Which is yet another reason to carefully and meticulously disclose all defects.)

But, perhaps during escrow the buyers found a different house and they now want out of your deal so they can buy it. They can create all sorts of fuss with the final walkthrough. I've seen cases where buyers have successfully used it as a tool to nix the deal and get their deposit back.

Sometimes agents try to avoid this problem by writing into the deposit receipt that the purpose of the final walkthrough is only to determine that the condition of the property hasn't changed—it's not a time to reopen negotiations. Unfortunately, the value of such clauses is debatable. And it might take a judge to sort it out.

Just keep in mind that in the vast majority of cases, buyers continue to want to buy your property through escrow. And any complaints they offer from the final walkthrough are usually minor . . . and often justified.

My own feeling is if problems arise here that are minor, I don't argue. I just fix them or pay for them. And escrow closes and the deal is completed.

A Done Deal

There's nothing so sweet as to receive word that title has been recorded in favor of the buyer . . . and that there's a check waiting for you at the escrow office.

Hopefully, the sale has been for the price you wanted—a good price. And the process was quick!

Congratulations! You're a proud seller. Now you can go out there and buy another house!

Index